THE MEDITATION
HANDBOOK

Also by Geshe Kelsang Gyatso

Meaningful to Behold
Clear Light of Bliss
Buddhism in the Tibetan Tradition
Heart of Wisdom
Universal Compassion
Joyful Path of Good Fortune
Guide to Dakini Land
The Bodhisattva Vow
Heart Jewel
Great Treasury of Merit
Introduction to Buddhism
Understanding the Mind
Tantric Grounds and Paths

THE MEDITATION HANDBOOK

Geshe Kelsang Gyatso

Tharpa Publications
London

First published as *A Meditation Handbook* 1990
Second edition totally reset 1993
Third edition 1995

Tharpa Publications
15 Bendemeer Road
London SW15 1JX

Cover painting of Buddha Shakyamuni
by the Tibetan artist Chating Jamyang Lama
Cover design by Stefan Killen
Cover photo of Geshe Kelsang Gyatso by Gerry Hale
Line illustrations by Andy Weber

British Library Cataloguing in Publication Data
Gyatso, Geshe Kelsang 1932–
The Meditation Handbook.
1. Mahayana Buddhism
Meditation – Manuals
I. Title
294.3422

ISBN 0 948006 44 7 – papercase
ISBN 0 948006 43 9 – paperback

Set in Palatino by Tharpa Publications
Printed on acid-free 250-year longlife paper and bound in
Great Britain by Redwood Books, Trowbridge, Wiltshire

Contents

Illustrations   vii
Acknowledgements   viii
Preface   ix
Editorial Note   xi

PART ONE: *Foundations and Preliminaries*
INTRODUCTION
What is Meditation?   3
The Objects of Meditation   4
Developing the Wish to Meditate   5
The Purpose of Meditation   6
Background Knowledge Required for Meditation   7
How to Meditate   12
THE PREPARATORY PRACTICES
Preparing for Meditation   16
The Preparatory Prayers   25

PART TWO: *The Twenty-one Meditations*
THE INITIAL SCOPE
   1 Relying upon a Spiritual Guide   31
   2 Our Precious Human Life   33
   3 Death and Impermanence   37
   4 The Danger of Lower Rebirth   41
   5 Refuge Practice   43
   6 Actions and their Effects   47

THE INTERMEDIATE SCOPE
   7 Developing Renunciation for Samsara   52

  8 Developing Equanimity   62
  9 Recognizing that all Living Beings are our
    Mothers   65
 10 Remembering the Kindness of Living Beings   69
 11 Equalizing Self and Others   73
 12 The Disadvantages of Self-cherishing   75
 13 The Advantages of Cherishing Others   79
 14 Exchanging Self with Others   83
 15 Great Compassion   85
 16 Taking   89
 17 Wishing Love   91
 18 Giving   95
 19 Bodhichitta   99
 20 Tranquil Abiding   101
 21 Superior Seeing   105
 Conclusion   117

Appendix I – A Special Breathing Meditation   119
Appendix II – The Commitments of Going for
    Refuge   125
Appendix III – A Suggested Retreat Schedule   133

Glossary   137
Bibliography   145
Study Programmes   148

Illustrations

Buddha Shakyamuni   2

The Seven Medicine Buddhas
Medicine Buddha   30
King of Clear Knowing   34
Melodious Ocean of Dharma Proclaimed   38
Supreme Glory Free from Sorrow   40
Stainless Excellent Gold   44
King of Melodious Sound   48
Glorious Renown of Excellent Signs   50

The Eight Bodhisattva Disciples of Buddha Shakyamuni
Avalokiteshvara   60
Manjushri   64
Vajrapani   68
Maitreya   72
Samantabhadra   78
Ksitigarbha   80
Sarvanivaranaviskambini   82
Akashagarbha   86

The Gurus of the Lamrim Lineage
Atisha   88
Dromtönpa   92
Geshe Potowa   94
Je Tsongkhapa   98
Je Phabongkhapa   102
Kyabje Trijang Rinpoche   106
Geshe Kelsang Gyatso Rinpoche   116

Acknowledgements

This text, *The Meditation Handbook*, is an important practical Buddhist meditation manual. It was written by Venerable Geshe Kelsang Gyatso during a meditation retreat at Tharpaland in Scotland. Our heartfelt gratitude goes to the author for his kindness in providing such clear guidelines to the spiritual path, and for presenting a straightforward way of integrating the vital practice of meditation into our daily lives.

The author was assisted in the initial stages of editing by Michael Garside. The full draft was passed on to Gen Thubten Gyatso for final editing, and checked closely by the author. It was then prepared for publication by Lucy James, Sherab Gyatso, and others in the Tharpa Editorial Office. Our thanks go to all of these dedicated students of the author for their excellent work.

May this priceless handbook bring the fruit of pure happiness to many beings.

Roy Tyson, Director
Manjushri Mahayana
Buddhist Centre
September 1993

Preface

The twenty-one meditation practices presented in this book are the essential practices of the stages of the path to enlightenment, or Lamrim in Tibetan. Lamrim is a special set of instructions that includes all the essential teachings of Buddha Shakyamuni, arranged in such a way that all his Hinayana and Mahayana teachings can be put into practice in a single meditation session. It was compiled by the great Indian Buddhist Master Atisha, who was invited to Tibet by King Jang Chub Ö in AD 1042, and who spent the rest of his life there spreading pure Dharma. There is a completely pure and unbroken lineage of these Lamrim instructions from Buddha Shakyamuni up to our present-day Spiritual Guides.

Many great Kadampa Teachers have said that it is far more important to gain experience of Lamrim than it is to attain clairvoyance, miracle powers, or high social status. This is true because in previous lives we have often possessed clairvoyance and potent miracle powers, and many times in the past we have been in the highest positions in the human and god realms, but despite this we continue to experience uncontrolled rebirth and physical and mental suffering caused by anger, attachment, jealousy, and confusion. If we gain deep experience of Lamrim there will be no basis for these problems; we shall be completely free from all of them.

First we must understand the value of Lamrim. Then by joyfully and patiently doing these meditations we shall gradually experience the fruits of Lamrim practice.

Eventually we shall attain freedom from all suffering, and the unchanging peace and happiness of full enlightenment.

Geshe Kelsang Gyatso
Tharpaland
November 1989

Editorial Note

Since this book is a manual for meditation practice, the explanations of the various Lamrim topics have been kept very concise. Those who wish to study Lamrim in more detail should study *Joyful Path of Good Fortune* by Geshe Kelsang Gyatso, which is an extensive commentary to all the meditations in this book.

PART ONE

Foundations and Preliminaries

Buddha Shakyamuni

Introduction

WHAT IS MEDITATION?

Meditation is a method for acquainting our mind with virtue. The more familiar our mind is with virtue, the calmer and more peaceful it becomes. When our mind is peaceful we are free from worries and mental discomfort, and we experience true happiness. If we train our mind to become peaceful we shall be happy all the time, even in the most adverse conditions but if our mind is not peaceful, then even if we have the most pleasant external conditions we shall not be happy. Therefore it is important to train our mind through meditation.

There are two types of meditation: analytical meditation and placement meditation. When we contemplate the meaning of a Dharma instruction we have heard or read we are doing analytical meditation. By deeply contemplating the instruction, eventually we reach a conclusion or cause a specific virtuous state of mind to arise. This is the object of placement meditation. Having found our object through analytical meditation, we then concentrate on it single-pointedly for as long as possible to become deeply acquainted with it. This single-pointed concentration is placement meditation. Often, analytical meditation is called simply 'contemplation' and placement meditation simply 'meditation'. Placement meditation depends upon contemplation, and contemplation depends upon listening to or reading Dharma instructions.

THE OBJECTS OF MEDITATION

In general, any virtuous object can be used as an object of meditation. If we discover that by acquainting our mind with a particular object our mind becomes more peaceful and virtuous, this indicates that for us that object is virtuous. If the opposite happens, for us it is a non-virtuous object. Many objects are neutral and have no particular positive or negative effect on our mind.

There are many different virtuous objects of meditation, but the most meaningful are those explained in this book – the visualization of the assembly of Buddhas and Bodhisattvas described on pages 19–20, and the objects of the twenty-one meditations, from meditation on relying upon a Spiritual Guide to meditation on emptiness, the ultimate nature of phenomena.

By relying upon a qualified Spiritual Guide we open the door to practising Dharma. Through the blessings of our Spiritual Guide we generate faith and confidence in our practice, and easily attain all the realizations of the stages of the path. For these reasons we need to meditate on relying upon a Spiritual Guide.

We need to meditate on our precious human life to realize that we now have a special opportunity to practise Dharma. If we appreciate the great potential of this life we shall not waste it by engaging in meaningless activities. We need to meditate on death and impermanence to overcome procrastination, and to ensure that our Dharma practice is pure by overcoming our preoccupation with worldly concerns. If we practise Dharma purely it is not very difficult to attain realizations. By meditating on the danger of lower rebirth, taking refuge sincerely, and avoiding non-virtue and practising virtue, we protect ourself from taking lower rebirth and ensure that life after life we shall obtain a precious human rebirth endowed with all the conditions conducive to the practice of Dharma.

We need to meditate on the sufferings of humans and gods so that we develop a spontaneous wish to attain permanent liberation, or nirvana. This wish, known as 'renunciation', strongly encourages us to complete the practice of the spiritual paths, which are the actual methods for attaining full liberation.

We need to meditate on love, compassion, and bodhichitta so that we can overcome our self-cherishing and develop and maintain a good heart towards all living beings. With this good heart we need to meditate on tranquil abiding and superior seeing so that we can eradicate our ignorance and finally become a Buddha by abandoning the two types of obstruction.

Besides these, there are many other objects of meditation. For example, if we wish to meditate on the breath, we can do so in conjunction with the practices of taking and giving explained on pages 89–90 and 95–7, or in conjunction with reciting the mantra of all Buddhas as explained in Appendix I. Both these meditations are very meaningful. If we devote too much time to ordinary breathing meditation we may find that we do not have enough time for our main practice, meditation on Lamrim.

DEVELOPING THE WISH TO MEDITATE

If we examine our life we shall probably discover that most of our time and energy is devoted to mundane activities, such as seeking material and emotional security, enjoying the pleasures of the senses, or establishing a good reputation. Although these things can make us happy for a short time, they are not able to provide the deep and lasting contentment we long for. Sooner or later our happiness turns into dissatisfaction, and we find ourself engaged in the pursuit of more worldly pleasures. Directly or indirectly, worldly pleasures cause us mental and physical suffering by stimulating attachment, jealousy, and frustration. Moreover, seeking to fulfil our own desires often brings us into conflict with others.

If true fulfilment cannot be found in worldly pleasures, where can it be found? Happiness is a state of mind, therefore the real source of happiness lies in the mind, not in external circumstances. If our mind is pure and peaceful we shall be happy, regardless of our external conditions, but if it is impure and unpeaceful we shall never find happiness, no matter how much we try to change our external conditions.

The purpose of Dharma practice is to cultivate those states of mind that are conducive to peace and well-being, and to eradicate those that are not. Only human beings can do this. Animals can enjoy food and sex, find homes, hoard wealth, subdue their enemies, and protect their family; but they cannot completely eliminate suffering and attain lasting happiness. It would be a great shame if we were to use our precious human life only to achieve results that even animals can achieve. If we wish to avoid such a wasted life and fulfil the real purpose of being born human we must devote ourself to the practice of Lamrim.

THE PURPOSE OF MEDITATION

According to the Lamrim instructions, we can engage in a meditation practice with any one of three levels of motivation. The first level, the motivation of the initial scope, is practising with the intention to protect ourself from the danger of taking lower rebirth by ensuring that in future lives we obtain a precious human rebirth endowed with all the conditions necessary for the practice of Dharma. The second level, the motivation of the intermediate scope, is practising with the intention to protect ourself from any kind of uncontrolled rebirth by attaining liberation from samsara. The third level, the motivation of the great scope, is practising with the intention to attain full enlightenment or Buddhahood so that we can benefit all living beings. These three levels of motivation are progressive. By engaging in meditation practices with the motivation of the initial scope we lay the foundation for advancing to the second level, and by engaging in meditation practices with the motivation of the intermediate scope we lay the foundation for advancing to the third level. All the essential practices of these three scopes are included within the twenty-one meditation practices presented in this book.

BACKGROUND KNOWLEDGE REQUIRED FOR MEDITATION

Since the meditations presented in this book assume a belief in rebirth, or reincarnation, a brief description of the process of death and rebirth, and the places in which we can be reborn, may be helpful.

The mind is neither physical, nor a by-product of purely physical processes, but is a formless continuum that is a separate entity from the body. When the body disintegrates at death the mind does not cease. Although our superficial conscious mind ceases, it does so by dissolving into a deeper level of consciousness, the very subtle mind; and the continuum of the very subtle mind has no beginning and no end. It is this mind which, when thoroughly purified, transforms into the omniscient mind of a Buddha.

Every action we perform leaves an imprint on our very subtle mind, and each imprint eventually gives rise to its own effect. Our mind is like a field, and performing actions is like sowing seeds in that field. Virtuous actions sow seeds of future happiness and non-virtuous actions sow seeds of future suffering. The seeds we have sown in the past remain dormant until the conditions necessary for their germination come together. In some cases this can be many lifetimes after the original action was performed.

The seeds that ripen when we die are very important because they determine what kind of rebirth we shall take. Which particular seed ripens at death depends upon the state of mind in which we die. If we die with a peaceful mind, this will stimulate a virtuous seed and we shall experience a fortunate rebirth, but if we die with an unpeaceful mind, in a state of anger, say, this will stimulate a non-virtuous seed and we shall experience an unfortunate rebirth. This is similar to the way in which nightmares are triggered off by our being in an agitated state of mind just before falling asleep.

The analogy of falling asleep is not accidental, for the process of sleep, dreaming, and waking closely resembles the process of death, intermediate state, and rebirth. When we fall asleep, our gross inner winds gather and dissolve inwards, and our mind becomes progressively more and more subtle until it transforms into the very subtle mind of the clear light of sleep. While the clear light of sleep is manifest we experience deep sleep, and to others we resemble a dead person. When it ends, our mind becomes gradually more and more gross and we pass through the various levels of the dream state. Finally, our normal powers of memory and mental control are restored and we wake up. When this happens, our dream world disappears and we perceive the world of the waking state.

A very similar process occurs when we die. As we die, our winds dissolve inwards and our mind becomes progressively more and more subtle until the very subtle mind of the clear light of death becomes manifest. The experience of the clear light of death is very similar to the experience of deep sleep. After the clear light of death has ceased, we experience the stages of the intermediate state, or bardo in Tibetan, which is a dream-like state that occurs between death and rebirth. After a few days or weeks, the intermediate state ends and we take rebirth. Just as when we wake from sleep the dream world disappears and we perceive the world of the waking state, so when we take rebirth the appearances of the intermediate state cease and we perceive the world of our next life.

The only significant difference between the process of sleep, dreaming, and waking and the process of death, intermediate state, and rebirth is that after the clear light of sleep has ceased the relationship between our mind and our present body remains intact, whereas after the clear light of death this relationship is broken.

While we are in the intermediate state we experience different visions that arise from the karmic seeds that were activated immediately before death. If negative seeds were activated these visions will be nightmarish, but if positive seeds were activated they will be predominantly pleasant. In either case, when the karmic seeds have matured sufficiently they impel us to take rebirth in one or other of the six realms of samsara.

The six realms are actual places in which we can be reborn. They are brought into existence through the power of our actions, or karma. There are three types of action: bodily actions, verbal actions, and mental actions. Since our bodily and verbal actions are initiated by our mental actions, ultimately the six realms are created by our mind. For example, a hell realm is a place that arises as a result of the worst actions, such as murder or extreme mental or physical cruelty, which depend upon the most deluded states of mind.

To form a mental image of the six realms we can compare them to the floors of a large, old house. In this analogy the house represents samsara, the cycle of death and rebirth that ordinary beings undergo without choice or control. The house has three storeys above ground, and three below. Deluded sentient beings are like the inhabitants of this house. They are continually moving up and down the house, sometimes living above ground, sometimes below.

The ground floor corresponds to the human realm. Above this, on the first floor, is the realm of the demi-gods, non-human beings who are continually at war with the gods. In terms of power and prosperity they are superior to humans, but they are so obsessed with jealousy and violence that their lives have little spiritual value.

On the top floor live the gods. The lower classes of gods, the desire realm gods, live a life of ease and luxury, devoting their time to enjoyment and the satisfaction of their desires. Though their world is a paradise and their lifespan is very long, they are not immortal and they eventually fall to lower states. Since their lives are filled with distractions it is difficult for them to find the motivation to practise Dharma. From a spiritual point of view a human life is much more meaningful than a god's life.

Higher than the desire realm gods are the gods of the form and formless realms. Having passed beyond sensual desire, the form realm gods experience the refined bliss of meditative absorption and possess bodies made of light. Transcending even these subtle forms, the gods of the formless realm abide without form in a subtle consciousness that resembles infinite space. Though their minds are the purest and most exalted within samsara, they have not overcome the ignorance of self-grasping, which is the root of samsara, and so, after experiencing bliss for many aeons, eventually their lives end and they are once again reborn in the lower states of samsara. Like the other gods they consume the merit they have created in the past and make little or no spiritual progress.

The three storeys above ground are called the 'fortunate realms' because the beings who inhabit them have relatively pleasant experiences which are caused by the practice of virtue. Below ground are the three lower realms, which are the result of negative bodily, verbal, and mental actions. The least painful of these is the animal realm, which in the analogy is the first floor beneath the ground. Included in this realm are all mammals apart from humans, as well as birds, fish, insects, worms – the whole animal kingdom. Their minds are characterized by extreme stupidity, without any spiritual awareness, and their lives by fear and brutality.

On the next floor down live the hungry ghosts. The principal causes of rebirth here are greed and negative actions motivated by miserliness. The consequence of these actions is extreme poverty. Hungry ghosts suffer continuous hunger and thirst which they are unable to satisfy. Their world is a vast desert. If by chance they come across a drop of water or a scrap of food it disappears like a mirage, or transforms into something repulsive such as pus or urine. These appearances are due to their negative karma and lack of merit.

The lowest floor is hell. The beings here experience unrelenting torment. Some hells are a mass of fire; others are desolate regions of ice and darkness. Monsters conjured up by the minds of the hell beings inflict terrible tortures on them. The suffering continues unremittingly for what seems an eternity, but eventually the karma that caused the beings to be born in hell is exhausted and the hell beings die and are reborn elsewhere in samsara.

This is a general picture of samsara. We have been trapped in samsara since beginningless time, wandering meaninglessly without any freedom or control, from the highest heaven to the deepest hell. Sometimes we dwell on the upper storeys with the gods; sometimes we find ourself on the ground floor with a human rebirth; but most of the time we are trapped in the underground floors experiencing terrible physical and mental suffering.

Although samsara resembles a prison, there is however one door through which we can escape. That door is emptiness, the ultimate nature of phenomena. By training in the spiritual paths described in this book we shall eventually find our way to this door, and, stepping through, discover that the house was simply an illusion, the creation of our impure mind. Samsara is not an external prison; it is a prison made by our own mind. It will never end by itself, but by diligently practising the true spiritual path and thereby eliminating our self-grasping and other delusions, we can bring our samsara to an end. Once we attain liberation ourself, we shall then be in a position to show others how to destroy their mental prison by eradicating their delusions.

If we practise the twenty-one meditations presented in this book we shall gradually overcome the deluded states of mind that keep us imprisoned in samsara, and develop all the qualities needed to attain full enlightenment. The first seven meditations function principally to help us to develop renunciation, the determination to escape from samsara. The next twelve meditations help us to cultivate heartfelt love and compassion for all living beings, and lead us to the realization that we can liberate others from samsara only by attaining enlightenment first. The principal obstacle that prevents us from attaining liberation and enlightenment is self-grasping, a deeply ingrained misconception of the way things exist. The main function of the last two meditations is to counter, and eventually to eradicate, this misconception.

HOW TO MEDITATE

Each of the twenty-one meditation practices has five parts: preparation, contemplation, meditation, dedication, and subsequent practice. The preparatory practices prepare our mind for successful meditation by purifying hindrances caused by our previous negative actions, empowering our mind with merit, and inspiring it with the blessings of the Buddhas and Bodhisattvas. These preparatory practices are performed at the beginning of each meditation session in conjunction with the short prayers found in the following chapter. It is useful to memorize these prayers. For those who are interested, an explanation of the prayers, as well as instructions on how to set up a shrine and sit in the correct meditation posture, are also given in the following chapter. If our meditation does not seem to be progressing, rather than becoming discouraged we should emphasize these preparatory practices purely and sincerely.

The second part of each practice is contemplation. The purpose of contemplation is to bring to mind the object of placement meditation. We do this by considering various lines of reasoning, contemplating analogies, and reflecting on the scriptures. It is helpful to memorize the contemplations given in each section so that we can meditate without having to look at the text. The contemplations given here are intended only as guidelines. We should supplement and enrich them with whatever reasons and examples we find helpful.

When through our contemplations the object appears clearly, we leave our analytical meditation and concentrate on the object single-pointedly. This single-pointed concentration is the third part, the actual meditation.

When we first start to meditate, our concentration is poor; we are easily distracted and often lose our object of meditation. Therefore, to begin with we shall probably need to alternate between contemplation and placement meditation many times in each session. For example, if we are meditating on compassion we begin by contemplating the various sufferings experienced by living beings until a strong feeling of compassion arises in our heart. When this feeling arises we meditate on it single-pointedly. If the feeling fades, or if our mind wanders to another object, we should return to analytical meditation to bring the feeling back to mind. When the feeling has been restored we once again leave our analytical meditation and hold the feeling with single-pointed concentration.

Both contemplation and meditation serve to acquaint our mind with virtuous objects. The more familiar we are with such objects, the more peaceful our mind becomes. By training in meditation and living in accordance with the insights and resolutions developed during meditation, eventually we shall be able to maintain a peaceful mind continuously, throughout our life. More detailed instructions on the contemplations and on meditation in general can be found in *Introduction to Buddhism, Joyful Path of Good Fortune*, and *Universal Compassion*.

The fourth part of each practice is dedication. Dedication directs the merit produced by our meditation towards the attainment of Buddhahood. If merit is not dedicated it can easily be destroyed by anger. By reciting the dedication prayers sincerely at the end of each meditation session we ensure that the merit we created by meditating is not wasted but acts as a cause for enlightenment.

The fifth part of each meditation practice is the subsequent practice. This consists of advice on how to integrate the meditation into our daily lives. It is important to remember that Dharma practice is not confined to our activities during the meditation session; it should permeate our whole life. We should not allow a gulf to develop between our meditation and our daily life, because the success of our meditation depends upon the purity of our conduct outside the meditation session. We should keep a watch over our mind at all times by applying mindfulness, alertness, and conscientiousness; and we should try to abandon whatever bad habits we may have. Deep experience of Dharma is the result of practical training over a long period of time, both in and out of meditation, therefore we should practise steadily and gently, without being in a hurry to see results.

To summarize, our mind is like a field. Engaging in the preparatory practices is like preparing the field by removing obstacles caused by past negative actions, making it fertile with merit, and watering it with the blessings of the holy beings. Contemplation and meditation are like sowing good seeds, and dedication and subsequent practice are the methods for ripening our harvest of Dharma realizations.

Lamrim instructions are not given merely for the sake of intellectual understanding of the path to enlightenment. They are given to help us to gain deep experience, and should therefore be put into practice. If we train our mind in these meditations every day, eventually we shall gain perfect realizations of all the stages of the path. Until we have reached this stage we should not tire of listening to oral teachings on Lamrim or reading authentic Lamrim commentaries, and then contemplating and meditating on these instructions. We need continually to expand our understanding of these essential topics and to use this new understanding to enhance our regular meditation.

If we genuinely wish to gain experience of the stages of the path we should try to meditate every day. On the first day we can meditate on relying upon a Spiritual Guide, on the second day on our precious human life, and so on, until we complete the whole cycle in twenty-one days. Then we can begin again. Between sessions we should try to remain mindful of the instructions on subsequent practice. Occasionally, when we have the opportunity, we should do a retreat on Lamrim. A suggested retreat schedule is given in Appendix III. By practising like this, we use our whole life to further our experience of the stages of the path.

The Preparatory Practices

PREPARING FOR MEDITATION

We all have the potential to gain realizations of each of the twenty-one meditation practices in this book. These potentials are like seeds in the field of our mind, and our meditation practice is like cultivating these seeds. However, our meditation practice will be successful only if we make good preparations beforehand.

If we want to cultivate external crops we begin by making careful preparations. First, we remove from the soil anything that might obstruct their growth, such as stones and weeds. Second, we enrich the soil with compost or fertilizer to give it the strength to sustain growth. Third, we provide warm, moist conditions to enable the seeds to germinate and the plants to grow. In the same way, to cultivate our inner crops of Dharma realizations we must also begin by making careful preparations. First, we must purify our mind to eliminate the negative karma we have accumulated in the past because if we do not purify this karma it will obstruct the growth of Dharma realizations. Second, we need to give our mind the strength to support the growth of Dharma realizations by accumulating merit. Third, we need to activate and sustain the growth of Dharma realizations by receiving the blessings of the holy beings.

It is very important to receive blessings. For example, if we are growing outer crops, even if we remove the weeds and fertilize the soil we shall not be able to grow anything if we do not provide warmth and moisture. These germinate the seeds, sustain the growth of the plants, and finally ripen the crop. In the same way, even if we purify our mind and accumulate merit we shall find it difficult to meet with success in our meditations if we do not receive the blessings of the holy beings. Receiving blessings transforms our mind by activating our virtuous potentials, sustaining the growth of our Dharma realizations, and bringing our Dharma practice to completion.

From this we can see that there are three essential preparations for successful meditation: purifying negativities, accumulating merit, and receiving blessings. The brief preparatory practices that now follow contain the essence of these three preparations.

Cleaning the environment

Before we sit down to meditate it is helpful to make sure that the place where we meditate is clean. A clean environment makes the mind clear and fresh. Moreover, during the preparatory practices we invite the Buddhas, Bodhisattvas, and other holy beings to come to our room as a Field for Accumulating Merit; and as a sign of respect we ensure that our room is clean and tidy beforehand.

Setting up a shrine

If possible we should set up a shrine with representations of Buddha's body, speech, and mind. To represent Buddha's body we place a statue or picture of Buddha in the centre of the shrine. To its right we place a Dharma text, representing Buddha's speech, and to its left we place a stupa, or a picture of a stupa, representing Buddha's mind. Remembering that Buddha's omniscient mind actually enters into these objects, we should feel that we are actually in the presence of the living Buddha and make prostrations and offerings accordingly.

If we like, we can set out actual offerings in front of the shrine, such as rows of seven water bowls, or anything clean and beautiful, such as flowers, incense, candles, honey, cakes, chocolate, or fruit. More information on setting up a shrine and making offerings can be found in *Joyful Path of Good Fortune*.

The meditation posture

When these preparations are completed we can sit down to meditate. If possible, we should sit in the vajra posture, but if we are unfamiliar with this we can sit in any posture that is comfortable. If we cannot sit cross-legged we can sit on a chair. The most important thing is to have a straight back so that the subtle energy winds in our body can flow freely and keep our mind alert. Our hands should rest just below the navel, with the palms open and facing upwards, the right hand above the left, and the two thumbs gently touching.

Calming the mind

Before beginning the actual preparatory prayers we should calm our mind by doing breathing meditation. Breathing naturally, we try to concentrate on our breath without being distracted by conceptual thoughts. As we breathe out we imagine that we exhale all our negativities, obstacles, and distracting thoughts in the form of black smoke. As we breathe in we imagine that we inhale the blessings of all the holy beings in the form of pure, white light. We continue with this meditation for a few minutes, or until our mind is calm and peaceful. If we like, we can use the special breathing meditation explained in Appendix I.

The remaining preparatory practices are done in conjunction with the brief prayers included at the end of this section. The purpose of reciting these prayers is to direct our mind to the particular practices. These will now be briefly explained.

Going for refuge We generate fear of the sufferings of samsara in general, and of rebirth in the lower realms in particular; and then, with strong faith that the Three Jewels have the power to protect us from these sufferings, we go for refuge to Buddha, Dharma, and Sangha while reciting the refuge prayer. The actual practice of going for refuge is explained in Meditation 5.

Generating bodhichitta There are two important things to emphasize when we meditate: our motivation at the beginning and our dedication at the end. We should begin by generating the motivation of bodhichitta, the wish to attain Buddhahood to help all living beings. With this motivation we recite the bodhichitta prayer. Our familiarity with both refuge and bodhichitta will naturally increase as we practise the cycle of twenty-one meditations.

Generating the four immeasurables These are four special states of mind that strengthen our bodhichitta. They are immeasurable love, the wish for all beings to be happy; immeasurable compassion, the wish for all beings to be free from suffering; immeasurable joy, the wish for all beings to attain the everlasting joy of liberation; and immeasurable equanimity, the wish for all beings to be free from unbalanced attitudes such as attachment and anger. They are called 'immeasurables' because we generate these minds while thinking of all living beings, who are immeasurable in number.

Visualizing the Field for Accumulating Merit The Field for Accumulating Merit is the assembly of Buddhas, Bodhisattvas, and other holy beings in whom we take refuge and to whom we make prostrations, offerings, confession, and so forth. We imagine that they are all in the space before us, with Buddha Shakyamuni, our main object of visualization, in the centre and all the other holy beings around him, like the full moon surrounded by stars. They are called a 'Field for Accumulating Merit' because by offering the prayer of seven limbs and the mandala to them we accumulate merit in our minds. At the beginning we should not expect to be able to visualize the whole assembly; it is sufficient simply to believe that they are all present before us.

Prayer of seven limbs The seven limbs are methods for purifying negativity and accumulating merit. They are: prostrating, making offerings, confessing non-virtue, rejoicing in virtue, beseeching the holy beings to remain, requesting Dharma teachings, and dedicating merit. They are called 'limbs' because they support our meditation, which is the main body of our practice. Prostrating, making offerings, rejoicing in virtue, beseeching the holy beings to remain, and requesting Dharma teachings all accumulate merit; confessing non-virtue purifies negativity; and dedicating our merit prevents our virtue from being destroyed.

To prostrate is to show respect. We can show respect with our body by making physical prostrations, or simply by placing our hands together at our heart; we can show respect with our speech by reciting verses of praise; and we can show respect with our mind by generating faith towards the holy beings. If possible we should make all three types of prostration together. This practice also serves to reduce our pride.

As already mentioned, we can make actual offerings by placing seven or more water bowls in front of our shrine, or by offering anything clean and beautiful, such as flowers, incense, or fruit. If we use our imagination we can offer jewelled palaces, gardens, scented bathing pools, even entire universes – all completely pure. The Buddhas and Bodhisattvas have no need for our offerings, but making extensive offerings has a very beneficial effect on our mind, creating a vast amount of merit and counteracting miserliness.

Confession enables us to purify negative actions committed in the past. If we sincerely contemplate and meditate on karma we shall realize that we have already committed countless heavy negative actions. Fearing the consequences of these actions, we develop a strong wish to purify them. To purify negative actions we must recognize the faults of these actions and feel regret for having committed them. Regret is not the same as guilt; it is simply a strong wish to purify our mind of the negative energy created by non-virtuous actions. Feeling regret for all the non-virtuous actions we have committed, we confess them to the holy beings. In this way we receive the purifying blessings of all the Buddhas and Bodhisattvas. With these attitudes of regret and faith, any virtuous actions we engage in serve as purification. If we begin every meditation session with sincere confession, the whole session serves to purify our accumulated negativity. To purify completely a non-virtuous action we must make a promise not to repeat it. There is little point in confessing our negative actions if we have no intention to refrain from committing them again in the future.

Rejoicing is to appreciate and rejoice in the virtues of ourself and others. Rejoicing in virtue increases our virtuous tendencies and overcomes jealousy and competitiveness. It is one of the easiest ways to create a vast amount of merit. Even lying in bed and rejoicing in the virtuous actions of others is a powerful spiritual practice.

Beseeching our Spiritual Guide and all the other holy beings to remain with us, to guide us and inspire us, helps us to keep a strong connection with our Spiritual Guide in this and future lives.

Requesting the holy beings to turn the Wheel of Dharma, that is, to give Dharma teachings, creates the cause for Dharma to remain in this world, and ensures that we shall meet with Dharma in our future lives.

As mentioned before, dedication is very important because it directs the merit we accumulate through our meditation practice towards the attainment of full enlightenment, and prevents it from being destroyed by anger or other non-virtuous minds such as wrong views. We dedicate by generating a strong mental intention that our merit will become a cause of our enlightenment for the benefit of all living beings.

For those who are interested in practising the seven limbs more elaborately, a detailed commentary can be found in *Joyful Path of Good Fortune* and in the second and third chapters of *Meaningful to Behold*.

Offering the mandala The mandala offering is a way to offer the entire universe in visualized form. We imagine that the whole universe transforms into a Buddha's Pure Land which we offer to the Field of Merit with the prayer that all living beings may soon come to live in such a Pure Land. To make the mandala offering we visualize that we hold in our hands a vast and circular golden base. In the centre stands Mount Meru, around this are four island continents, and in the space above are the sun and the moon. Everything pure and beautiful is included in the mandala. When we recite the second verse of the mandala offering we offer everything that stimulates our delusions. We imagine that the people and things to which we are attached, as well as those that cause us to develop hatred and confusion, all transform into pure beings and enjoyments, and we offer them to the Three Jewels. By transforming and offering the objects of the three poisons, attachment, hatred, and confusion, we remove the basis upon which these delusions develop. More detail on offering the mandala can be found in *Joyful Path of Good Fortune*, *Great Treasury of Merit*, and *Guide to Dakini Land*.

Prayer of the Stages of the Path After purifying negativity and accumulating merit by reciting the prayer of seven limbs and offering the mandala, we now request the holy beings to grant their blessings so that we may receive all the realizations of the stages of the path. We make this request by reciting the *Prayer of the Stages of the Path* while concentrating single-pointedly on its meaning.

Receiving blessings and purifying After making requests by reciting the *Prayer of the Stages of the Path* we imagine that Buddha Shakyamuni and all the other Buddhas and Bodhisattvas are delighted. Smiling with the love of a father for his dearest child, Buddha radiates rays of light and nectar from his heart which enter the crown of our head and fill our whole body. This purifies all our hindrances to attaining deep experience of the topic on which we are about to meditate, and makes our mind very clear, positive, and powerful. We should firmly believe that this happens.

Contemplation and meditation Now that we have purified our mind, accumulated merit, and received blessings, we are ready to begin our contemplation and meditation by following the specific instructions given for each meditation.

If during the course of our meditation our mind becomes dull or heavy, or if we meet with other difficulties, we should pause from our meditation and make prayers to the holy beings in front of us. We imagine that they answer our prayers with powerful lights and nectars which flow into our body and immediately dispel our obstacles. We then resume our meditation.

These preparations are extremely important for success-ful meditation. If we wish to spend longer on them, we can recite a slightly more extensive preparatory prayer called *Essence of Good Fortune*, which can be found in *Joyful Path of Good Fortune*. If we wish, we can emphasize going for refuge by reciting the refuge prayer hundreds of times, or we can accumulate merit by making many man-dala offerings, or we can emphasize purification by mak-ing prostrations to the Thirty-five Confession Buddhas, as explained in the book *The Bodhisattva Vow*. Sometimes, if we wish, we can devote the entire session to the pre-paratory practices.

Dedication At the end of our session we imagine that all the holy beings melt into light and dissolve through the crown of our head. We feel as if our body, speech, and mind have become one with Buddha's body, speech, and mind. Then, while reciting the dedication prayers, we dedicate the merit we have accumulated from practising the preparations, contemplating, and meditating to the happiness of all living beings.

THE PREPARATORY PRAYERS

Going for refuge

We imagine ourself and all other living beings going for refuge while reciting three times:

I and all sentient beings, until we achieve enlightenment,
Go for refuge to Buddha, Dharma, and Sangha.

(3x, 7x, 100x, or more)

Generating bodhichitta

Through the virtues I collect by giving and other
 perfections,
May I become a Buddha for the benefit of all.   (3x)

Generating the four immeasurables

May everyone be happy,
May everyone be free from misery,
May no one ever be separated from their happiness,
May everyone have equanimity, free from hatred and
 attachment.

Visualizing the Field for Accumulating Merit

In the space before me is the living Buddha Shakyamuni
surrounded by all the Buddhas and Bodhisattvas, like the
full moon surrounded by stars.

Prayer of seven limbs

With my body, speech, and mind, humbly I prostrate,
And make offerings both set out and imagined.
I confess my wrong deeds from all time,
And rejoice in the virtues of all.
Please stay until samsara ceases,
And turn the Wheel of Dharma for us.
I dedicate all virtues to great enlightenment.

Offering the mandala

The ground sprinkled with perfume and spread with
    flowers,
The Great Mountain, four lands, sun and moon,
Seen as a Buddha Land and offered thus,
May all beings enjoy such Pure Lands.

I offer without any sense of loss
The objects that give rise to my attachment, hatred,
    and confusion,
My friends, enemies, and strangers, our bodies and
    enjoyments;
Please accept these and bless me to be released directly
    from the three poisons.

IDAM GURU RATNA MANDALAKAM NIRYATAYAMI

Prayer of the Stages of the Path

The path begins with strong reliance
On my kind Teacher, source of all good;
O Bless me with this understanding
To follow him with great devotion.

This human life with all its freedoms,
Extremely rare, with so much meaning;
O Bless me with this understanding
All day and night to seize its essence.

My body, like a water bubble,
Decays and dies so very quickly;
After death come results of karma,
Just like the shadow of a body.

With this firm knowledge and remembrance
Bless me to be extremely cautious,
Always avoiding harmful actions
And gathering abundant virtue.

Samsara's pleasures are deceptive,
Give no contentment, only torment;
So please bless me to strive sincerely
To gain the bliss of perfect freedom.

O Bless me so that from this pure thought
Come mindfulness and greatest caution,
To keep as my essential practice
The doctrine's root, the Pratimoksha.

Just like myself all my kind mothers
Are drowning in samsara's ocean;
O So that I may soon release them,
Bless me to train in bodhichitta.

But I cannot become a Buddha
By this alone without three ethics;
So bless me with the strength to practise
The Bodhisattva's ordination.

By pacifying my distractions
And analyzing perfect meanings,
Bless me to quickly gain the union
Of special insight and quiescence.

When I become a pure container
Through common paths, bless me to enter
The essence practice of good fortune,
The supreme vehicle, Vajrayana.

The two attainments both depend on
My sacred vows and my commitments;
Bless me to understand this clearly
And keep them at the cost of my life.

By constant practice in four sessions,
The way explained by holy Teachers,
O Bless me to gain both the stages
Which are the essence of the Tantras.

May those who guide me on the good path
And my companions all have long lives;
Bless me to pacify completely
All obstacles, outer and inner.

May I always find perfect Teachers
And take delight in holy Dharma,
Accomplish all grounds and paths swiftly,
And gain the state of Vajradhara.

Receiving blessings and purifying

From the hearts of all the holy beings, streams of light
and nectar flow down, granting blessings and purifying.

*At this point we begin the actual contemplation and medi-
tation. After the meditation we dedicate our merit while
reciting the following:*

Dedication prayers

Through the virtues I have collected
By practising the stages of the path,
May all living beings find the opportunity
To practise in the same way.

May everyone experience
The happiness of humans and gods,
And quickly attain enlightenment,
So that samsara is finally extinguished.

PART TWO

―――――

The Twenty-one Meditations

Medicine Buddha

The Initial Scope

1. RELYING UPON A SPIRITUAL GUIDE

Relying sincerely upon a qualified Spiritual Guide is the foundation for all spiritual attainments. In this meditation we generate a strong determination to rely upon a Spiritual Guide by considering the many benefits we shall experience.

PREPARATION

First we go for refuge, generate a special bodhichitta motivation, and complete the other preparatory practices by reciting the brief prayers on pages 25–8.

CONTEMPLATION

We think 'If I rely sincerely upon a Spiritual Guide, he or she will lead me along the spiritual path, which is the only way I can solve all my problems and make my life meaningful. I shall gradually draw closer to the attainment of full enlightenment. All the Buddhas will be delighted with me. I shall be protected from harm caused by humans or non-humans. I shall find it easy to abandon delusions and non-virtuous actions. My practical experience of the spiritual path will increase. I shall never be born in lower realms. In all my future lives I shall meet well-qualified Spiritual Guides. All my virtuous wishes for beneficial conditions within samsara, as well as for liberation and enlightenment, will be fulfilled.'

MEDITATION

We contemplate these benefits until we generate the determination to rely upon a Spiritual Guide sincerely and with strong faith. We meditate on this determination for as long as possible.

DEDICATION

We dedicate all the virtues we have created by engaging in the preparatory practices, contemplating, and meditating, to the welfare of all living beings by reciting the dedication prayers on page 28.

SUBSEQUENT PRACTICE

During the meditation break we should try to please our Spiritual Guide by sincerely putting his or her instructions into practice. We should improve our faith in him and, in particular, try to prevent negative thoughts towards him. If we wish to practise Dharma but have not yet met a Spiritual Guide, we should be encouraged by the determination made during the meditation to search for a qualified Spiritual Guide who can teach us the stages of the path and guide us towards enlightenment.

2. OUR PRECIOUS HUMAN LIFE

By doing this meditation we shall come to realize that this human life is very precious because it provides us with a special opportunity to practise Dharma. Once we realize this we shall make a strong determination not to waste our life, but to use it to practise Dharma purely.

PREPARATION

We go for refuge, generate a special bodhichitta motivation, and complete the other preparatory practices as before.

FIRST CONTEMPLATION

Countless living beings take rebirth as animals, hungry ghosts, and hell beings. Because these beings experience continuous, unimaginable sufferings in the lower realms, none of them has the opportunity to practise Dharma. Among those who are born as human beings there are many who have no opportunity to listen to or practise Buddha's teachings. Millions of people live in countries where religion is not tolerated. Some people hold wrong views denying rebirth, the law of karma, or the existence of enlightened beings. Many people are physically or mentally handicapped, or incapacitated by accidents. Others suffer extreme poverty and deprivation, or are caught up in wars or natural disasters. None of these people has the opportunity to follow the spiritual path. Realizing this, we should think 'Unlike all these poor beings, I am free from all these impediments. I am very fortunate. I have an opportunity to listen to instructions on Buddhadharma and put them into practice. I have faith in these instructions. I have complete mental and physical faculties, and it is easy for me to find all the other conditions that are necessary for practising Dharma.'

King of Clear Knowing

FIRST MEDITATION

We contemplate these points until we generate a feeling of deep appreciation for the preciousness of our human life, seeing that it provides all the conditions necessary for spiritual practice. We think 'I am very fortunate', and then meditate on this feeling single-pointedly.

SECOND CONTEMPLATION

We think 'If I use this human life well by practising Dharma, I shall be able to overcome all the problems of this life and protect myself from falling into a lower rebirth in the future. If I practise the stages of the path of the intermediate scope I shall become free from uncontrolled rebirth and attain the peace of liberation; and if I practise the stages of the path of the great scope I shall attain full enlightenment and be able to benefit all living beings. My human life is a real wishfulfilling jewel because it enables me to fulfil my principal wish – to free myself and others from every kind of suffering so that we can experience real happiness. It is only with this human form that I can fulfil this wish.'

SECOND MEDITATION

We contemplate these points until we generate the determination 'I will use this precious human life to practise Dharma without wasting even a single moment.' We then meditate on this determination single-pointedly.

DEDICATION

We dedicate all the virtues we have created in this meditation practice to the welfare of all living beings by reciting the dedication prayers.

SUBSEQUENT PRACTICE

During the meditation break we try never to lose our appreciation of the preciousness of our human life. If we keep this in mind all the time we shall always maintain a happy mind and never become discouraged, whatever our external circumstances. Reflecting on the preciousness of our human life will encourage us not to waste valuable time, but to use it to practise the stages of the path.

3. DEATH AND IMPERMANENCE

There are three ways in which we can make our human life meaningful: by using it to ensure that we take rebirth as a human or a god in our next life, by using it to attain liberation from samsara, or by using it to attain full enlightenment for the benefit of others. These attainments depend upon the practice of Dharma, but because we are so attached to worldly activities we do not have a strong wish to practise Dharma. This is our main obstacle. To overcome this obstacle we need to meditate on death.

PREPARATION

We go for refuge, generate a special bodhichitta motivation, and complete the other preparatory practices.

CONTEMPLATION

We think 'I shall definitely die. There is no way to prevent my body from finally decaying. Day by day, moment by moment, my life is slipping away. I have no idea when I shall die; the time of death is completely uncertain. Many young people die before their parents; some die the moment they are born – there is no certainty in this world. Furthermore, there are so many causes of untimely death. The lives of many strong and healthy people are destroyed by accidents. There is no guarantee that I shall not die today.'

MEDITATION

After contemplating these points we mentally repeat over and over again 'I may die today, I may die today', and concentrate on the feeling it evokes. Eventually we shall come to a conclusion 'Since I shall soon have to depart from this world, there is no sense in my becoming

Melodious Ocean of Dharma Proclaimed

attached to worldly enjoyments. Instead, I will devote my whole life to the practice of Dharma.' We then meditate on this conclusion for as long as we can.

DEDICATION

We dedicate all the virtues we have created in this meditation practice to the welfare of all living beings by reciting the dedication prayers.

SUBSEQUENT PRACTICE

During the meditation break we should try to practise Dharma without laziness. Realizing that worldly pleasures are deceptive and that they distract us from using our life in a meaningful way, we should abandon attachment to them. In this way we can eliminate the main obstacle to pure Dharma practice.

Supreme Glory Free from Sorrow

4. THE DANGER OF LOWER REBIRTH

When we die, if the karma that ripens is negative we shall take rebirth in one of the lower realms. By meditating on this danger we develop a strong fear of the sufferings of the lower realms. This fear is one of the main causes of going for refuge.

PREPARATION

We go for refuge, generate a special bodhichitta motivation, and complete the other preparatory practices.

CONTEMPLATION

When the oil of an oil lamp is exhausted the flame goes out because the flame is produced from the oil, but when our body dies our consciousness is not extinguished because consciousness is not produced from the body. When we die our mind has to leave this present body, which is just a temporary abode, and find another body, rather like a bird leaving one nest to fly to another. Our mind has no freedom to remain and no choice about where to go. We are blown to the place of our next rebirth by the winds of our karma. If the karma that ripens at our death time is negative, we shall definitely take a lower rebirth. Heavy negative karma causes rebirth in hell, less negative karma causes rebirth as a hungry ghost, and the least negative karma causes rebirth as an animal.

It is very easy to commit heavy negative karma. For example, simply by swatting a mosquito out of anger we create the cause to be reborn in hell. Throughout this and all our countless previous lives we have committed many heavy negative actions. Unless we have already purified these actions by practising sincere confession, their potentialities remain in our mental continuum, and any one of these negative potentialities could ripen when we die. Bearing this in mind, we should ask ourself 'If I die today, where shall I be tomorrow? It is quite possible that I shall find myself in the animal realm, among the hungry ghosts, or in hell. If someone were to call me a stupid cow today I would find it difficult to bear, but what shall I do if I actually become a cow, a pig, or a fish?'

MEDITATION

We contemplate the sufferings of the three lower realms, and the danger of being reborn there, until we generate a strong fear of taking rebirth in the lower realms. We then meditate on this feeling of fear for as long as possible.

DEDICATION

We dedicate all the virtues we have created in this meditation practice to the welfare of all living beings by reciting the dedication prayers.

SUBSEQUENT PRACTICE

During the meditation break we should not forget the danger of taking a lower rebirth. This helps us to maintain mindfulness, and to be conscientious in avoiding non-virtuous actions. We are also inspired to seek refuge in the Three Jewels, which is the actual protection from suffering.

5. REFUGE PRACTICE

Having developed fear by contemplating the danger of lower rebirth, we now consider how the Three Jewels, Buddha, Dharma, and Sangha, have complete power to protect us.

We go for refuge, generate a special bodhichitta motivation, and complete the other preparatory practices.

Since all the fears and dangers of samsara, including rebirth in the lower realms, arise from our deluded minds, our real refuge is Dharma, the spiritual realizations that directly protect us from delusions. For example, if we gain a realization of death and impermanence this will help us to reduce our attachment to the things of this life. If we have strong awareness of the inevitability of death and the uncertainty of its time we shall naturally value the practice of moral discipline more than the pursuit of transitory sense pleasures, wealth, or power. We shall not be tempted to commit non-virtuous actions such as killing, stealing, or sexual misconduct, and so we shall not have to experience the unpleasant consequences of such actions. This is how Dharma realizations protect us from suffering. The ultimate Dharma refuge is the realization of emptiness. This permanently eradicates all our delusions and frees us once and for all from suffering.

Whereas Dharma is the actual refuge, Buddha is the source of all refuge. He is the supreme Spiritual Guide who shows us the way to attain Dharma realizations and who sustains our Dharma practice by bestowing his blessings. The Sangha are the supreme spiritual friends who support our Dharma practice. They provide conducive

Stainless Excellent Gold

conditions, encourage us in our practice, and set a good example for us to follow. Only the Three Jewels have the ability to protect living beings from all suffering.

MEDITATION

By thinking in this way we generate a strong conviction that the Three Jewels are the only true objects of refuge, and we develop deep faith in Buddha, Dharma, and Sangha. We meditate on this without allowing any doubts to arise.

When we meditate on a mental attitude such as faith, we do not merely think about it and focus on it as if it were separate from our mind; rather we transform our mind into that state and hold it single-pointedly. We should feel as if our mind has merged with an ocean of faith.

After meditating on our faith in the Three Jewels for a short time, we imagine that in front of us is the living Buddha Shakyamuni surrounded by all the Buddhas and Bodhisattvas, like the full moon surrounded by stars. We generate a strong conviction that all these holy beings are actually present before us and focus on them for a while. Fearing rebirth in the lower realms and having deep faith in the Three Jewels, we generate a strong determination to build the foundation of the Dharma Jewel within our mind by relying upon the Buddha Jewel and the Sangha Jewel. With this motivation we make the following request:

All Buddhas, Bodhisattvas, and holy beings,
Please protect me and all living beings
From the various sufferings, fears, and dangers of
samsara.
Please bestow your blessings upon our body and mind.

We recite this refuge prayer many times with deep faith in the Three Jewels.

DEDICATION

We dedicate all the virtues we have created in this meditation practice to the welfare of all living beings by reciting the dedication prayers.

SUBSEQUENT PRACTICE

During the meditation break we should practise the twelve commitments of refuge which are explained in detail in Appendix II. Keeping the refuge commitments helps us to strengthen our refuge practice so that it will quickly bear fruit.

6. ACTIONS AND THEIR EFFECTS

Having gone for refuge, our main practice is to observe the laws of karma by abandoning non-virtue and practising virtue. This is the actual method for protecting ourself from rebirth in the lower realms, and the foundation of all other Dharma realizations.

PREPARATION

We go for refuge, generate a special bodhichitta motivation, and complete the other preparatory practices.

CONTEMPLATION

The main cause of rebirth in the lower realms is non-virtuous actions, or negative karma. All the suffering we experience in this life, such as sickness, poverty, conflict, accidents, and harm from humans and non-humans, is the result of our own past negative karma. If our dearest wishes remain unfulfilled while the things we dislike appear with ease, or if we fail to find good friends, or, having found them, we are soon separated from them, these too are due to the ripening of our past negative karma. Even minor annoyances such as interferences in our daily routine, or the discontent that underlies so much of our life, are the result of the non-virtuous actions accumulated in previous lives. Conversely, our precious human life, all the happiness experienced by humans and gods, and the attainments of liberation and enlightenment are the result of virtuous actions.

This dependent relationship between actions and their effects, virtuous actions causing happiness and non-virtuous actions causing suffering, is taught by the Buddhas based on their perfect knowledge. We must believe it because conviction in the laws of karma is the root of future happiness.

King of Melodious Sound

MEDITATION

We contemplate these points until we develop conviction in the truth of karma. Then we make the determination 'Since I wish to be free from every misfortune and enjoy uninterrupted happiness, I must abandon non-virtuous actions and practise only virtue. In particular, I must abandon the ten non-virtuous actions.' We then make this determination firm by meditating on it with single-pointed concentration.

DEDICATION

We dedicate all the virtues we have created in this meditation practice to the welfare of all living beings by reciting the dedication prayers.

SUBSEQUENT PRACTICE

During the meditation break we should conscientiously avoid even small negative actions and practise whatever virtuous actions we can. In this way we shall be able to overcome our immediate problems and protect ourself from future suffering. Practising moral discipline purely makes our human life meaningful. It is the only infallible method for solving our inner problems.

Glorious Renown of Excellent Signs

The Intermediate Scope

Since beginningless time we have taken countless rebirths without interruption due to our self-grasping. This cycle of uninterrupted death, intermediate state, and rebirth is known as samsara. As long as we remain trapped in samsara we shall experience only suffering.

Going for refuge to the Three Jewels, combined with the practice of pure moral discipline, will free us from the danger of lower rebirth and enable us to obtain a precious human life again in the future. However, even in the human realm we are not free from suffering, and there is no real happiness. We have only to look around us, read a newspaper, or watch television to see that human beings experience terrible sufferings.

Wherever we are born in samsara, even in the highest god realm, there is no freedom from suffering. If we succeed in taking rebirth in the fortunate realms it is only like taking a short holiday. Afterwards we once again have to descend to the lower realms, where we experience extreme suffering for inconceivably long periods.

We experience all these sufferings because we are in samsara. If we think deeply about this we shall realize that if we want real freedom and real happiness we must escape from samsara. By practising the stages of the path of the intermediate scope we can escape from samsara and attain permanent inner peace, with complete freedom from all suffering, fears, and their causes. This is real liberation, or nirvana.

7. DEVELOPING RENUNCIATION FOR SAMSARA

Since the root cause of samsara is self-grasping, to escape from samsara we must cut this root by eradicating self-grasping from our mental continuum. This depends upon training in higher wisdom, which depends upon training in higher concentration, which depends upon training in higher moral discipline. These three trainings are called 'higher' trainings because they are motivated by renunciation, the wish to escape from samsara. Therefore, our first step in escaping from samsara is to develop a spontaneous realization of renunciation.

We develop renunciation by contemplating the many faults of samsara and generating a strong wish to escape. In the following contemplations we think about the various sufferings experienced in the human realm, but we should bear in mind that the sufferings of other realms are generally far worse.

We may wonder why it is necessary to contemplate sufferings such as birth, ageing, sickness, and death, especially since we have already experienced the first and can do nothing to avoid the others. The reason is that by meditating on these sufferings we realize that the very nature of samsaric existence is suffering, and that until we escape from samsara we shall have to experience the same pains in life after life. This induces a strong wish to escape from samsara by abandoning its cause, self-grasping. This wish is renunciation.

PREPARATION

We go for refuge, generate a special bodhichitta motivation, and complete the other preparatory practices.

CONTEMPLATION

There now follow seven separate contemplations on the sufferings of samsara, each of which is designed to generate a mind of renunciation, which we then take as the object of meditation. It is not necessary to contemplate all these points in each session. Rather we should contemplate mainly those points that have the greatest impact on our mind and that help us to develop renunciation. When renunciation arises in our mind we should refrain from further contemplation and proceed to the meditation.

Birth

We have to spend the first nine months of our life cramped inside our mother's womb. At the beginning the rapid growth of our limbs makes us feel as if we are being stretched out on a rack, and in the later months of pregnancy we feel as if we are squashed inside a small water tank full of filthy liquid. We are extremely sensitive to everything our mother does. For example, if she runs, our fragile body is severely jolted, and if she drinks anything hot it feels like boiling water scalding our skin. During all this time we are completely alone. Our mother does not know the suffering and fear that we experience and, even if she did, she would be powerless to help us.

When we finally emerge from the womb it is like being forced through a narrow crevice between two hard rocks into a harsh and alien world. We have forgotten all we knew in our previous life, and have no way of understanding what is now happening to us. It is as if we are blind, deaf, and dumb. Our skin is so tender that even the softest clothes feel abrasive. When we are hungry we cannot say 'I need food', and when we are in pain we cannot say 'This is hurting me.' The only signs we can make are hot tears and furious gestures. We are completely helpless and have to be taught everything – how to eat, how to sit, how to walk, how to talk.

Ageing

As we grow old, our youthful vitality diminishes. We become bent, ugly, and burdened with illness. Our eyesight becomes weaker and our hearing fails. We cannot derive the same enjoyment from the things we used to enjoy, such as food, drink, and sex. We are too weak to play games, and we are often too exhausted even for entertainments. When we are young we can travel around the whole world, but when we are old we can hardly walk to our own front door. We become too weak to engage in many worldly activities, and our spiritual activities are often curtailed. For example, we cannot make many prostrations or travel far to receive teachings. If we meditate we find it harder to gain realizations because our memory and concentration are weak and we find it difficult to stay awake. Our intellect is less sharp than it was during our youth, and so when we try to study it takes much longer to understand things.

Unable to do the work we used to do, or to help others in the way we would like to, we begin to feel useless to society and start to lose our self-respect. We are often neglected by our own children, and we watch helplessly as one by one our friends and contemporaries grow sick and die. Inexorably our loneliness deepens. If we did not practise Dharma while we were younger and had the opportunity, we pass our few remaining years with a growing fear of death, and a deepening sense of regret for a wasted life.

Sickness

Having been born human, it is almost impossible to escape having to experience sickness in this life. When we fall ill we are like a bird that has been soaring in the sky and is suddenly shot down. When a bird is shot, it falls straight to the ground like a lump of lead and all its glory and power are immediately destroyed. Even a mild illness can be completely incapacitating. We cannot enjoy the food we like or take part in the activities of our friends. We may be told that we must never again eat our favourite food, drink alcohol, or engage in strenuous exercise. If our disease is more serious we may have to undergo painful and possibly risky operations. Should these fail, we shall be told that the doctors can do nothing to cure us and that we have only a short time left to live. If we have not used our life to practise Dharma we shall be overcome by fear and regret.

Young people in their prime may be struck down by an incurable degenerative illness and, though they remain alive for many years, they will have to watch themselves slowly deteriorate. Realizing that their most treasured hopes and dreams will never be fulfilled they may wish they could die sooner. When we hear or read about the horrible diseases experienced by others we must remember that the same could happen to us. While we remain in samsara we are never safe from the threat of sickness.

Death

If during our life we have worked hard to acquire possessions and have become very attached to them, we shall experience great suffering when we are separated from them at the time of death. Even now we find it difficult to lend one of our most treasured possessions to someone else, let alone to give it away. No wonder we become so miserable when we realize that in the hands of death we must abandon everything.

When we die we have to part from even our closest friends. We have to leave our partner, even though we may have been together for many years and never spent a day apart. If we are very attached to our friends we shall experience great misery at the time of death, but all we shall be able to do is to hold their hands. We shall not be able to halt the process of death, even if they plead with us not to die. Usually when we are very attached to someone we feel jealous if they leave us on our own and spend time with someone else, but when we die we shall have to leave our friends with others forever. If we have children we shall have to leave them when we die. We shall have to leave our Spiritual Guides and all the people who have helped us in this life.

When we die, this body that we have cherished and cared for in so many ways will have to be left behind. It will become mindless like a stone and will be buried in the ground or cremated. If we have not practised Dharma and cultivated virtuous actions, at the time of death we shall experience fear and distress, as well as bodily pain.

Having to part with what we like

Before the final separation at the time of death, we often have to experience temporary separation from the people and things we like. We may have to leave our country where all our friends and relatives live, or we may have to leave the job we like. We may lose our reputation. Many times in this life we have to experience the misery of parting from the people we like, or forsaking and losing the things we find pleasant and attractive, but when we die we have to part forever from all the companions and enjoyments of this life.

Having to encounter what we do not like

We are often forced to live or work with people whom we find unpleasant, such as those who criticize us for no reason, or with those who continually interfere with our wishes. Sometimes we may find ourself in very dangerous situations such as in a fire or an earthquake, or attacked by a mugger or a rapist. If our country goes to war we may be called up to fight, or be imprisoned if we refuse. Our homes may be bombed and our relatives killed. Our lives are full of less extreme situations which we find annoying. On holiday it rains, but back in the office the heat is stifling. Our business fails, or we lose our job, or we use up all our savings. We argue with our partner, our children cause us many worries, and old friends suddenly turn against us. Whatever we do, something always seems to go wrong. Even in our Dharma practice we continually meet obstacles. When we sit down to meditate we are distracted by outside noise, the telephone rings, or someone comes to see us. Sometimes it seems that even though we have been practising Dharma for years our delusions are stronger than ever. Even though we try so hard to be considerate, sometimes our family or our friends become unhappy about our Dharma practice. It is as if we are living in a thorn bush – whenever we adjust ourself to make ourself more comfortable, the thorns only pierce us more deeply. In samsara, aggravation and frustration are the natural state of affairs.

Failing to satisfy our desires

We have countless desires. Many cannot be fulfilled at all and others, when fulfilled, do not bring us the satisfaction for which we hoped. Many people are unable to satisfy even modest desires for the basic necessities of life such as adequate food, clothing, shelter, companionship, tolerable work, or a degree of personal freedom. Unfortunately, even if these basic needs are met, our desires do not end there. Soon we need a car, a more luxurious home, a better-paid job. In the past a simple holiday at the seaside may have been sufficient, but our expectations continually increase and now we need expensive, foreign holidays.

Ambition and competitiveness are a common cause of dissatisfaction. The ambitious schoolchild cannot rest content until he or she comes top of the class, nor the businessman until he has made his fortune. Clearly not everyone can come top. For one person to win, others must lose, but even the winners are rarely satisfied for long; their ambition drives them on until they too are beaten, worn out, or dead.

Another reason why we fail to satisfy all our desires is that they are often contradictory. For example, we may want both worldly success and a simple life, or fame and privacy, or rich food and a slim figure, or excitement and security. We may demand our own way all the time and still expect to be popular, or we may wish for Dharma realizations yet still covet a good reputation and material wealth. Our desires often involve other people, and this creates special complications. Many relationships break up because of unrealistic expectations and desires.

We seek perfection – the perfect society, the perfect home, the perfect partner – but perfection cannot be found in samsara. Samsara promises much but can never deliver real satisfaction. It is not possible for impure, transient objects to provide the lasting joy we seek. This can be attained only by thoroughly purifying our mind. Ignorance is the fundamental cause of samsara, but worldly desires are the fuel that perpetuates it. Therefore we need to reduce our worldly desires by recognizing their faults.

MEDITATION

By contemplating these seven types of suffering we shall come to the conclusion 'I have experienced these sufferings over and over again in the past and, if I do not attain liberation, I shall have to experience them over and over again in the future. Therefore I must escape from samsara.'

When this thought arises clearly and definitely in our mind we meditate on it for as long as possible.

DEDICATION

We dedicate all the virtues we have created in this meditation practice to the welfare of all living beings by reciting the dedication prayers.

SUBSEQUENT PRACTICE

Throughout the meditation break we should maintain the wish to attain liberation from samsara. When we meet with difficult circumstances or see others experiencing difficulties, we should use these to remind ourself of the disadvantages of samsara. When things are going well we should not be deceived but recall that samsaric pleasures are short-lived and ensnare us if we become attached to them. In this way we can use all our experiences of daily life to strengthen our determination to escape from samsara and attain liberation.

Avalokiteshvara

The Great Scope

We should maintain the wish to escape from samsara day and night. It is the main path to liberation and the basis of more advanced realizations. However, we should not be content with seeking merely our own liberation; we need also to consider the welfare of other living beings. There are countless beings trapped in the prison of samsara experiencing an unlimited variety of sufferings. Whereas each one of us is just one single person, other people are countless in number; therefore the happiness of others is much more important than our own happiness. For this reason we must enter the Mahayana path, the supreme method for benefiting all living beings.

8. DEVELOPING EQUANIMITY

Our attitudes towards others are normally unbalanced. When we see a friend or someone we find particularly attractive we feel pleased, when we see an enemy or an unattractive person we feel dislike for them, and when we see a stranger or someone we find neither attractive nor unattractive we feel indifference. Such unbalanced attitudes are the main obstacle to developing unbiased love, compassion, and bodhichitta, which are the essential realizations of the Mahayana. For as long as we have these attitudes our mind will be like a rocky field which cannot support the growth of Mahayana realizations. Our first task, therefore, is to free our mind from these unbalanced attitudes and develop a genuine equanimity towards all living beings.

PREPARATION

We go for refuge, generate a special bodhichitta motivation, and complete the other preparatory practices.

CONTEMPLATION

We should think that in previous lives the person who is now our friend was often our enemy, while our present enemy has often been our closest friend. Even within one short life, friends quickly turn into enemies and enemies turn into friends. There is no certainty. Moreover, in the past we have been close to those we now regard as strangers, and there will come a time when we shall become estranged from those to whom we now feel close. Therefore, there is no sense in our being attached to some and feeling aversion or indifference towards others. By thinking in this way we can give up these unbalanced attitudes of attachment, aversion, and indifference, and cultivate instead a feeling of warmth towards all living beings.

MEDITATION

By contemplating these points we arrive at three resolutions:

1 I will free my mind from unbalanced attitudes.
2 I will not feel attachment, aversion, or indifference towards any living being.
3 I will develop and maintain a warm and friendly attitude towards all living beings equally.

We meditate single-pointedly on these three resolutions for as long as possible.

DEDICATION

We dedicate all the virtues we have created in this meditation practice to the welfare of all living beings by reciting the dedication prayers.

SUBSEQUENT PRACTICE

We should maintain these three resolutions day and night, keeping in our heart a warm feeling towards everyone we meet or think about. If we do this there will be no basis for the problems of attachment or anger to arise, and our mind will remain at peace all the time.

Manjushri

9. RECOGNIZING THAT ALL LIVING BEINGS ARE OUR MOTHERS

Having generated equanimity, we now need to generate love, compassion, and bodhichitta. These depend upon first generating affectionate love for all living beings. To generate affectionate love we begin by contemplating how all living beings are our mothers.

PREPARATION

We go for refuge, generate a special bodhichitta motivation, and complete the other preparatory practices.

CONTEMPLATION

Since it is impossible to find a beginning to our mental continuum it follows that we have taken countless rebirths in the past, and if we have had countless rebirths we must have had countless mothers. Where are all these mothers now? They are all the living beings alive today.

It is incorrect to reason that our mothers of former lives are no longer our mothers just because a long time has passed since they actually cared for us. If our present mother were to die today, would she cease to be our mother? No, we would still regard her as our mother and pray for her happiness. The same is true of all our previous mothers – they died, yet they remain our mothers. It is only because of the changes in our external appearance that we do not recognize each other.

In our daily life we see many different living beings, both human and non-human. We regard some as friends, some as enemies, and most as strangers. These distinctions are made by our mistaken minds; they are not verified by valid minds. As a result of the different karmic relationships we have had in the past, some living beings now appear to us to be attractive, some unattractive, and others neither particularly attractive nor unattractive. We tend to assent to these appearances unquestioningly, as if they were really true. We believe that those who now appear pleasant are intrinsically pleasant people, while those whom we find unattractive are actually unpleasant. This way of thinking is clearly incorrect. If the people whom we find attractive were intrinsically pleasant, everyone who met them would find them pleasant; and if the people whom we find unattractive were intrinsically unpleasant, everyone who met them would find them unpleasant; but this is not the case. Therefore, rather than following such mistaken minds, it would be better to regard all living beings as our mothers. Whoever we meet, we should think 'This person is my mother.' In this way we shall feel equally warm towards all living beings.

If we regard all living beings as our mothers we shall find it easy to develop pure love and compassion, our everyday relationships will become pure and stable, and we shall naturally avoid negative actions such as killing or harming living beings. Since it is so beneficial to regard all living beings as our mothers, we should adopt this way of thinking without hesitation.

MEDITATION

We contemplate in this way until we develop the conviction that all beings are our mothers. Then we meditate on this conviction single-pointedly to make it firm.

DEDICATION

We dedicate all the virtues we have created in this meditation practice to the welfare of all living beings by reciting the dedication prayers.

SUBSEQUENT PRACTICE

In between sessions we should regard everyone we meet as our mother. This applies even to animals and insects, as well as to our enemies. Instead of identifying people as friends, enemies, or strangers, we should try to view them all equally as being our mother. In this way we shall overcome the harmful attitudes of attachment, hatred, and indifference.

Vajrapani

10. REMEMBERING THE KINDNESS OF LIVING BEINGS

Having become convinced that all living beings are our mothers, we now contemplate their kindness to generate a feeling of affectionate love towards them. In this meditation we begin by contemplating the immense kindness we have received from each living being when they were our mother, and then we contemplate and meditate on the kindness they have shown us at other times.

PREPARATION

We go for refuge, generate a special bodhichitta motivation, and complete the other preparatory practices.

CONTEMPLATION

When we were conceived, had our mother not wanted to keep us in her womb she could have had an abortion. If she had done so we would not now have this human life. Through her kindness she allowed us to stay in her womb, and so we now enjoy a human life and experience all its advantages. When we were a baby, had we not received her constant care and attention we would certainly have had an accident and could now be handicapped, crippled, or blind. Fortunately our mother did not neglect us. Day and night she gave us her loving care, regarding us as more important than herself. She saved our life many times each day. During the night she allowed her sleep to be interrupted, and during the day she forfeited her usual pleasures. She had to leave her job, and when her friends went out to enjoy themselves she had to stay behind. She spent all her money on us, giving us the best food and the best clothes she could afford. She taught us how to eat, how to walk, how to talk. Thinking of our future welfare, she did her best to ensure that we received a good education. Due to her kindness we are now able to study whatever we choose. It is principally through the kindness of our mother that we now have the opportunity to practise Dharma and eventually to attain enlightenment.

Since there is no one who has not been our mother at some time in our previous lives, and since when we were their child they treated us with the same kindness as our present mother has treated us in this life, all living beings are very kind.

The kindness of living beings is not limited to the times when they have been our mother. All the time, our day-to-day needs are provided through the kindness of others. We brought nothing with us from our former life, yet as soon as we were born we were given a home, food, clothes, and everything we needed – all provided through the kindness of others. Everything we now enjoy has been provided through the generosity of other beings, past or present.

We are able to make use of many things with very little effort on our own part. If we consider facilities such as roads, cars, trains, aeroplanes, ships, houses, restaurants, hotels, libraries, hospitals, shops, money, and so on, it is clear that many people worked very hard to provide these things. Even though we make little or no contribution towards the provision of these facilities, they are all available for us to use. This shows the great kindness of others.

Both our general education and our spiritual training are provided by others. All our Dharma realizations, from our very first insights up to our eventual attainment of liberation and enlightenment, will be attained in dependence upon the kindness of others.

MEDITATION

We contemplate the great kindness of mother living beings until we develop a deep sense of gratitude. We then meditate on this feeling single-pointedly.

DEDICATION

We dedicate all the virtues we have created in this meditation practice to the welfare of all living beings by reciting the dedication prayers.

SUBSEQUENT PRACTICE

Throughout all our activities we should maintain the recognition that all beings are very kind to us. This special way of viewing living beings will prevent us from becoming involved in arguments or from criticizing others. We shall easily attain the realizations of love, compassion, and bodhichitta.

Maitreya

11. EQUALIZING SELF AND OTHERS

To equalize self and others is to cherish others as much as we cherish ourself. Until now we have cherished only ourself. The aim of this meditation is to share our feeling of cherishing so that we come to cherish ourself and all living beings equally.

PREPARATION

We go for refuge, generate a special bodhichitta motivation, and complete the other preparatory practices.

CONTEMPLATION

We think 'There are three correct reasons why I should cherish myself and others equally:

1 All living beings have shown me great kindness in both this and previous lives.
2 Just as I wish to be free from suffering and experience only happiness, so do all other beings. In this respect I am no different from any other being; we are all equal.
3 I am only one, whereas others are countless, so how can I cherish myself alone while I neglect to cherish others? My happiness and suffering are insignificant when compared with the happiness and suffering of all other living beings.'

MEDITATION

We contemplate these three reasons until a determination to cherish others as much as we cherish ourself arises strongly in our mind. We then meditate on this determination for as long as possible.

DEDICATION

We dedicate all the virtues we have created in this meditation practice to the welfare of all living beings by reciting the dedication prayers.

SUBSEQUENT PRACTICE

Whenever we meet someone, or think of someone, we should remember the determination we made in the meditation session and cherish them sincerely. We should feel affectionate love for all living beings and always value their happiness and freedom. If we train in this way many of the problems we experience in daily life will disappear, because most of our problems arise from regarding ourself as more important than others.

12. THE DISADVANTAGES OF SELF-CHERISHING

We usually regard ourself as especially precious and important, and feel that our own happiness matters most. This attitude, which is known as 'self-cherishing', is a great obstacle to developing great compassion and bodhichitta. In this meditation we generate a strong determination to overcome our self-cherishing by considering its many faults and disadvantages.

PREPARATION

We go for refuge, generate a special bodhichitta motivation, and complete the other preparatory practices.

CONTEMPLATION

Motivated by self-cherishing we perform many negative actions – bodily, verbal, and mental. As a result of these negative actions we experience suffering and misfortune. All suffering, all fear, and all unfulfilled wishes are the result of negative karma, and all negative karma arises from self-cherishing.

If we hear even the slightest criticism we immediately feel pain because our self-cherishing mind wishes to hear only those things that make us feel comfortable. All our unhappiness, depression, and mental discomfort come from self-cherishing.

If a mother living being such as a poor, hungry mouse were to come into our room searching for food, we would probably become unhappy, and instead of generating compassion we might even become angry. This is because our self-cherishing regards only ourself as important and has no wish to benefit others.

It is generally assumed that self-cherishing is necessary for survival, and that it is only because we cherish ourself that we look after ourself at all. On the surface this seems to be true, but if we think more deeply, taking into account the laws of karma, we shall realize that the opposite is the case. It is the self-cherishing we harbour in our hearts that is responsible for all our problems and that constantly destroys our well-being, even threatening our very survival. For example, some people become so disappointed or angry when their wishes are not fulfilled that they kill themselves. Such anger or despair arises only from strong attachment to one's own happiness, so indirectly self-cherishing is responsible even for suicide. Nothing causes us greater harm than this demon of self-cherishing; it is the source of all negativity and all misfortune.

We do not need self-cherishing to look after ourself, or to survive. If we regard our body as being in the service of others, we can eat, wash, work, rest, and so on without self-cherishing. Moreover, people who genuinely love others and have an unselfish, undemanding disposition are generally well-liked and readily receive assistance from others.

MEDITATION

We contemplate these points until we develop a strong determination to abandon our self-cherishing. Then we meditate single-pointedly on this determination.

DEDICATION

We dedicate all the virtues we have created in this meditation practice to the welfare of all living beings by reciting the dedication prayers.

SUBSEQUENT PRACTICE

We should be ever mindful of the faults of self-cherishing and, by repeatedly recalling the determination we made in meditation, we should try gradually to abandon it.

Whenever we experience difficulties or suffering we should not blame other people or the external situation – rather we should remember that ultimately all our problems arise from self-cherishing. Therefore, when things go wrong we should blame only our self-cherishing mind. By practising in this way our self-cherishing, the root of all faults, will gradually diminish and eventually cease altogether.

Samantabhadra

13. THE ADVANTAGES OF CHERISHING OTHERS

Previously we generated affectionate love for all mother living beings. On the basis of this we now need to generate cherishing love, a mind that regards all living beings as important and feels them to be very special. In this meditation we generate a strong determination to cherish others by contemplating the many advantages of so doing.

PREPARATION

We go for refuge, generate a special bodhichitta motivation, and complete the other preparatory practices.

CONTEMPLATION

If we think clearly we shall realize that all our present and future happiness depends upon our cherishing others. How is this? In our past lives, because we cherished others, we practised moral discipline such as refraining from killing or harming others, and abandoning stealing from them. Sometimes out of fondness for them we practised giving and patience. As a result of these positive actions we have now obtained this precious human life. Moreover, because sometimes in the past we helped others and gave them protection, we ourself now receive help and enjoy pleasant conditions.

If we sincerely practise cherishing others we shall experience many benefits in this and future lives. The immediate effect will be that many of our problems such as those that arise from anger and jealousy will disappear, and our mind will become calm and peaceful. Since we shall act in a considerate way, we shall please others and not become involved in quarrels or disputes. If we cherish others we shall be concerned not to harm them, so we shall naturally avoid negative actions. Instead, we shall practise positive actions such as love, patience, and

Ksitigarbha

generosity, and thus create the cause to gain a precious human life in the future.

If we make cherishing others our main practice, we shall gradually develop very special minds of great compassion and bodhichitta, and as a result we shall eventually come to enjoy the ultimate happiness of full enlightenment.

MEDITATION

We contemplate these points until we arrive at the decision 'I must always cherish other beings because this precious mind of love will bring happiness to myself and others.' We then hold this thought and meditate on it single-pointedly for as long as possible.

DEDICATION

We dedicate all the virtues we have created in this meditation practice to the welfare of all living beings by reciting the dedication prayers.

SUBSEQUENT PRACTICE

During the meditation break we should continue to keep in mind the advantages of cherishing others, and gradually improve our consideration, respect, and love for them.

Sarvanivaranaviskambini

14. EXCHANGING SELF WITH OTHERS

Exchanging self with others means changing the object of our cherishing so that we give up cherishing ourself and cherish only others.

PREPARATION

We go for refuge, generate a special bodhichitta motivation, and complete the other preparatory practices.

CONTEMPLATION

Since beginningless time we have cherished only ourself. So strong has been our self-cherishing that we have never forgotten our own welfare for a moment, even during sleep. Again and again this attitude has caused us to create the karma to be reborn in samsara and experience relentless suffering.

Buddha himself, and many of his followers, have understood the disadvantages of self-cherishing and the advantages of cherishing others. They have realized that the main cause of the ultimate happiness of Buddhahood is exchanging self with others. Therefore they have abandoned self-cherishing, and have come to regard the happiness of all other living beings as supremely important, dedicating all their actions to the welfare of others. The result is that they have attained full enlightenment and have been able to rescue many living beings from the sufferings of samsara.

MEDITATION

We contemplate these points until we gain a deep understanding of them. Finally we come to the conclusion 'I must abandon self-cherishing and cherish only others because self-cherishing is the source of all suffering and the root of samsara, and cherishing others is the source of all happiness and the root of liberation and full enlightenment.' When this determination arises in our mind we meditate on it single-pointedly.

DEDICATION

We dedicate all the virtues we have created in this meditation practice to the welfare of all living beings by reciting the dedication prayers.

SUBSEQUENT PRACTICE

By remaining mindful of the determination made in meditation, we should try not to follow our instinctive self-cherishing but instead try to cherish others. When we are familiar with exchanging self with others we shall become like the great Tibetan Bodhisattva, Geshe Langri Tangpa, who was able to accept happily any pain or difficulty such as illness, loss, or criticism, and to offer all his success and good conditions to others.

15. GREAT COMPASSION

Having developed cherishing love for all living beings, we now contemplate their suffering so that we can generate compassion for them. For this meditation we imagine that our parents of this life are beside us, and that they are surrounded by all living beings of the six realms. To help us visualize them we can imagine them all in human aspect, but we should remember that in reality they are beings of the six realms experiencing their own particular sufferings.

PREPARATION

We go for refuge, generate a special bodhichitta motivation, and complete the other preparatory practices.

CONTEMPLATION

None of these poor beings around me wants to suffer. They all long to be free, but they do not know how to escape. They are confused about the real causes of suffering, so they cannot find the means to abandon it. Out of ignorance they continually perform actions that cause them to be reborn in samsara. It seems as if their misery has no end.

Because they have taken rebirth in samsara, all these beings are experiencing continuous suffering. For example, human beings are experiencing unbearable human suffering. Without any choice they have to experience the sufferings of birth, ageing, sickness, and death. Again and again they have to part with what they like and encounter what they do not like. They are never able to satisfy their desires, but experience constant disappointment and frustration.

If we recall our contemplations on these seven sufferings from the meditation on renunciation and now apply

Akashagarbha

them to others, we shall realize that all human beings are experiencing constant suffering. We can increase our awareness of human suffering by recalling tragedies that we ourself have witnessed, read about, or seen on television.

The suffering of animals is a hundred times worse than human suffering, and the suffering experienced by hungry ghosts is even worse. The most severe and long-lasting suffering is that experienced by hell beings.

Although the gods and demi-gods generally enjoy better physical conditions than do humans, even they are not free from mental suffering, and in the future they will once again have to experience the immense sufferings of the lower realms.

MEDITATION

We contemplate these points until there arises in our mind a strong feeling of compassion for all living beings. We generate the compassionate wish 'How wonderful it would be if all living beings were free from suffering', and meditate on this wish for as long as possible.

DEDICATION

We dedicate all the virtues we have created in this meditation practice to the welfare of all living beings by reciting the dedication prayers.

SUBSEQUENT PRACTICE

During the meditation break we should try to maintain a compassionate heart day and night. Whenever we see or hear of others' suffering we should try to strengthen our compassion. We must also try to help in practical ways wherever possible. For example, we can rescue animals whose lives are in danger, comfort those who are distressed, or relieve the pain of those who are sick.

Atisha

16. TAKING

Having developed the compassionate wish for all living beings to be freed from their suffering, we must now realize that it is not enough merely to wish for this to happen; we must personally take responsibility for making it happen.

PREPARATION

We go for refuge, generate a special bodhichitta motivation, and complete the other preparatory practices.

CONTEMPLATION

We begin by generating the superior intention 'I myself will liberate all beings from their suffering.' Motivated by this superior intention we pray 'May all the suffering, fears, and obstacles of every living being ripen upon me, and may they thereby be freed from all problems.' We then imagine that all their sufferings, fears, and obstacles gather in the aspect of black smoke which dissolves into our heart, destroying our self-cherishing mind and freeing all living beings from their suffering.

MEDITATION

We develop strong conviction that all living beings have actually been released from their suffering and that our self-cherishing mind has been completely destroyed. With this conviction we generate a feeling of great joy. We take this feeling of joy as our object of meditation and hold it with single-pointed concentration for as long as possible.

DEDICATION

We dedicate all the virtues we have created in this meditation practice to the welfare of all living beings by reciting the dedication prayers.

SUBSEQUENT PRACTICE

During the meditation break we should put our compassionate intention into practice by alleviating others' suffering whenever we can. In this way we increase both our compassion and our merit. We should patiently accept whatever misfortune befalls us and use our own suffering as an example to help us develop sympathy for others. By practising in these ways our self-cherishing will gradually diminish and we shall develop the courage actually to take on the suffering of others.

17. WISHING LOVE

In this meditation we once again imagine ourself surrounded by all living beings, with our parents closest to us. We then recall from our previous meditations the love that cherishes all beings equally. With this mind we contemplate how all the beings around us have no real happiness. This naturally gives rise to the wish for them to find pure happiness. This wish is called 'wishing love'.

PREPARATION

We go for refuge, generate a special bodhichitta motivation, and complete the other preparatory practices.

CONTEMPLATION

Although all these beings desire real happiness they do not know how to obtain it. Instead of engaging in actions that cause real happiness they destroy whatever merit they have by getting angry, holding wrong views, or committing other negative actions.

No one in samsara enjoys real happiness. The happiness experienced by samsaric beings is simply worldly pleasure, which in reality is the suffering of change. In samsara all pleasures are short-lived and eventually change into pain. For example, the worldly pleasure we experience in ordinary relationships is not real happiness, but a temporary diminishment of our loneliness. Sooner or later, problems arise in our relationship, or it comes to an end. Our pleasures never last.

We generally assume that rich people must experience true happiness because they can enjoy all the pleasures and luxuries we would like to enjoy, but the pleasure they experience is, in reality, merely a temporary reduction of the suffering of discontent which arises from their unfulfilled desires.

Dromtönpa

MEDITATION

We contemplate these points until we generate a sincere wish 'How wonderful it would be if all beings could experience true happiness!' We take this mind of wishing love as our object of meditation and hold it single-pointedly.

DEDICATION

We dedicate all the virtues we have created in this meditation practice to the welfare of all living beings by reciting the dedication prayers.

SUBSEQUENT PRACTICE

During the meditation break we should maintain wishing love day and night by constantly reminding ourself that these living beings whom we cherish so much have no true happiness. When our hearts are filled with pure love we cannot be disturbed by anger or jealousy.

Geshe Potowa

18. GIVING

Having generated the wish for all living beings to be happy, we now train in actually giving them happiness.

PREPARATION

We go for refuge, generate a special bodhichitta motivation, and complete the other preparatory practices.

CONTEMPLATION

We begin by generating the intention 'Since I wish for all beings to enjoy true happiness, I must act to make this really happen.' With this motivation we imagine that our body transforms into a wishfulfilling jewel from which light radiates and illuminates all six realms. From this light, humans receive whatever they desire, animals are freed from danger, hungry ghosts receive food and drink, beings in the cold hells receive warmth, and a cooling breeze refreshes those in the hot hells. Demi-gods are granted protection, and gods are blessed with uncontaminated happiness.

MEDITATION

We generate a strong conviction that as a result of our practice of giving, all living beings experience an uncontaminated happiness and are completely satisfied. With this conviction we generate a special feeling of joy. We then meditate on this feeling for as long as possible.

Once we have become familiar with the practices of taking and giving as explained here, we can combine them by mounting them on the breath. To do this we must have the correct motivation of compassion and love for all beings. Breathing naturally, we imagine that when we breathe in we inhale, in the form of black smoke, all the suffering, delusions, and negative karma of all living beings. This black smoke enters through our nostrils and descends to our heart where it completely destroys our self-cherishing mind. As a result our mind transforms into uncontaminated bliss and our body becomes the pure body of a Buddha. As we breathe out we exhale white light which blesses the minds of all living beings and grants them whatever they desire or need. We repeat this visualization with each inhalation and exhalation.

Since there is quite a lot to visualize in a short space of time, it is difficult to do this practice if we are not already familiar with the basic meditations on taking and giving. Once these are mastered, however, this practice is an exceptionally powerful method for developing and increasing our compassion, love, and bodhichitta.

The breath and the mind are closely related. If the breath is harnessed for virtuous purposes it will gradually become pure, and as a result our mind will gradually become peaceful. Since we breathe all the time, if we use this method to keep our breath pure we shall easily be able to maintain peaceful and virtuous states of mind all the time.

More elaborate instructions on taking and giving can be found in the book *Universal Compassion*.

DEDICATION

We dedicate all the virtues we have created in this meditation practice to the welfare of all living beings by reciting the dedication prayers.

SUBSEQUENT PRACTICE

During the meditation break we should try to practise giving material things, giving Dharma, and giving fear-lessness. Whenever we can, we should try to be of service to others. We should also make prayers and dedicate our merit so that all living beings obtain pure happiness. In this way our wishing love as well as our merit will increase.

Je Tsongkhapa

19. BODHICHITTA

The eleven meditations from equanimity to giving are the actual methods for developing bodhichitta. In general, there are two methods for developing bodhichitta: the method of the sevenfold cause and effect, and the method of equalizing and exchanging self with others. The system presented here is a synthesis of these two traditions. Through improving our experience of these meditations we generate a special bodhichitta. In particular, the superior intention generated through taking and giving directly induces an especially powerful bodhichitta. This is defined as a primary mind spontaneously wishing to attain Buddhahood for the sake of all living beings that is motivated by the special superior intention arising from exchanging self with others.

PREPARATION

We go for refuge, generate a special bodhichitta motivation, and complete the other preparatory practices.

CONTEMPLATION

We recall the superior intention generated in the meditation on taking and think 'I have assumed responsibility for liberating all living beings from suffering, but how can I do this without first attaining enlightenment myself? Only a Buddha has the power to protect all living beings and to bestow upon them uncontaminated bliss. Therefore, to fulfil my wish to liberate others from their suffering I must become a Buddha.'

MEDITATION

When by contemplating in this way we arrive at the conclusion 'I must attain Buddhahood for the benefit of all', we hold it single-pointedly for as long as possible. If the thought begins to fade we renew it by repeating the contemplation.

DEDICATION

We dedicate all the virtues we have created in this meditation practice to the welfare of all living beings by reciting the dedication prayers.

SUBSEQUENT PRACTICE

We should try to maintain bodhichitta day and night. In particular, we should try to ensure that whatever actions we undertake are motivated by bodhichitta. In this way all our actions become powerful causes of Buddhahood.

Having gained some experience of bodhichitta, we should bring it to completion by practising the three higher trainings of the Mahayana: training in the perfection of moral discipline by keeping the Bodhisattva vows purely; training in the perfection of mental stabilization by striving to attain tranquil abiding; and training in the perfection of wisdom by developing superior seeing.

20. TRANQUIL ABIDING

To release our mind from self-grasping, the root of all delusions, we need a direct realization of emptiness. This depends upon tranquil abiding. Without tranquil abiding our mind is unstable, like a candle flame exposed to the wind, and so we are not able to realize clearly and directly subtle objects such as emptiness. It is not just the direct realization of emptiness that depends upon tranquil abiding; we also need tranquil abiding to attain pure clairvoyance, miracle powers, and spontaneous realizations of renunciation and bodhichitta.

In general, whenever we experience pure concentration on any of the objects of the twenty-one meditations our mind abides in a tranquil state, free from distractions. This is the function of pure concentration. However, actual tranquil abiding is a special concentration that is attained by completing the training in the nine levels of concentration – known as the 'nine mental abidings' – and which is conjoined with a special bliss of mental and physical suppleness. To train in tranquil abiding we first need to choose an object of meditation. We can use any one of the objects of the twenty-one meditations. If we choose an object such as equanimity, love, compassion, or bodhichitta, we first transform our mind into that particular state of mind by using the appropriate contemplations, and then hold that state of mind with single-pointed concentration. If we choose an object such as emptiness, impermanence, or the preciousness of this human life, we first attain a clear mental image of the object by relying upon the appropriate contemplations, and then concentrate single-pointedly on that image.

When we are training in tranquil abiding we have to overcome five major faults: laziness, forgetfulness, sinking and excitement, non-application, and application. To do this we have to train in the eight opponents: faith,

Je Phabongkhapa

aspiration, effort, suppleness, mindfulness, alertness, application, and non-application. These are explained in detail in *Joyful Path of Good Fortune*.

The instructions that follow explain how to begin to train in tranquil abiding using great compassion as the object. If you choose a different object you can modify the instructions accordingly.

PREPARATION

We go for refuge, generate a special bodhichitta motivation, and complete the other preparatory practices.

CONTEMPLATION

By recalling our previous meditations, we first bring to mind the love that cherishes all other living beings. With this mind we then think deeply about the suffering experienced by these poor beings. When as a result of these contemplations a strong feeling of compassion arises in our mind, we have found our object of tranquil abiding meditation.

MEDITATION

Having transformed our mind into compassion, we now stop contemplating and hold this mind with strong concentration. This is the first of the nine mental abidings. When the object fades, or our mind wanders to another object, we return to the contemplations to bring the object back to mind. Then once again we discontinue our contemplations and hold the object with single-pointed concentration. We continue in this way, alternating between contemplation and meditation, for the rest of the session.

We continue to improve our concentration in this way until we are able to remain concentrated on our object for five minutes. At this point we shall have advanced to the second mental abiding. By improving our concentration we shall gradually progress through the nine mental abidings and eventually attain tranquil abiding itself. At this point, although we still have the body of a human being, our mind will be the mind of a form realm god.

DEDICATION

We dedicate all the virtues we have created in this meditation practice to the welfare of all living beings by reciting the dedication prayers.

SUBSEQUENT PRACTICE

The principal practice during the meditation break is carefully to observe pure moral discipline by relying upon mindfulness and conscientiousness. In this way we avoid distracting entanglements that obstruct our training in tranquil abiding. Again and again we should think about the benefits of attaining tranquil abiding to increase our enthusiasm for the practice; and to improve our understanding we should read authentic instructions on tranquil abiding such as those found in *Joyful Path of Good Fortune* and *Meaningful to Behold*.

Once we have attained the fourth mental abiding we are ready to do a strict retreat on tranquil abiding. In some cases, at this stage it is possible to attain actual tranquil abiding within six months. For our retreat on tranquil abiding to be successful we need to find a suitable place which is very quiet and has all the necessary conditions. We must have few desires and be able to remain content all the time. During the retreat we should refrain from worldly activities and keep moral discipline purely, thereby reducing distracting conceptions. In brief, we must free ourself from all obstacles to developing concentration, and obtain all conducive internal and external conditions.

21. SUPERIOR SEEING

Superior seeing is a wisdom accomplished after the attainment of tranquil abiding that is held by a special bliss of suppleness produced by analyzing the nature of the object. The principal object of superior seeing is emptiness; therefore in this section we emphasize meditation on emptiness.

Emptiness is not nothingness, but lack of inherent existence. Inherent existence is mistakenly projected onto phenomena by our self-grasping mind. All phenomena naturally appear to our mind to be inherently existent and, without realizing that this appearance is mistaken, we instinctively assent to it and hold phenomena to exist inherently, or truly. This is the fundamental reason why we are in samsara.

There are two stages to realizing emptiness. The first stage is clearly to identify the way phenomena appear to our mind to be inherently existent, and how we firmly believe in the truth of this appearance. This is called 'identifying the object of negation'. If our meditation on emptiness is to be effective it is essential that we begin with a very clear image of what is to be negated. The second stage is to refute the object of negation, that is, to prove to ourself using various lines of reasoning that the object of negation does not actually exist. In this way we shall come to realize the absence, or non-existence, of the object of negation, which is emptiness.

Because we grasp most strongly at ourself and our body, we should begin by contemplating the emptiness of these two phenomena. We can do this by training in the two meditations explained below: meditation on the emptiness of the I, and meditation on the emptiness of the body.

Kyabje Trijang Rinpoche

We go for refuge, generate a special bodhichitta motivation, and complete the other preparatory practices.

The emptiness of the I

Identifying the object of negation

Although we grasp at an inherently existent I all the time, even during sleep, it is not easy to identify how it appears to our mind. To identify it clearly we must begin by allowing it to manifest strongly by contemplating situations in which we have an exaggerated sense of I, such as when we are embarrassed, ashamed, afraid, or indignant. We recall or imagine such a situation and then, without any comment or analysis, try to attain a clear mental image of how the I naturally appears at such times. We have to be patient at this stage because it may take many sessions before we attain a clear image. Eventually we shall see that the I appears to be completely solid and real, existing from its own side without depending upon the body or the mind. This vividly appearing I is the inherently existent I that we cherish so strongly. It is the I that we defend when we are criticized, and that we are so proud of when we are praised.

Once we have an image of how the I appears in these extreme circumstances, we should try to identify how it appears normally, in less extreme situations. For example, we can observe the I that is presently meditating and try to discover how it appears to our mind. Eventually we shall see that although in this case there is not such an inflated sense of I, nevertheless the I still appears to be inherently existent, existing from its own side without depending upon the body or the mind.

Once we have an image of the inherently existent I, we focus on it for a while with single-pointed concentration, and then we proceed to the second stage.

Refuting the object of negation

If the I exists in the way that it appears, it must exist in one of four ways: as the body, as the mind, as the collection of the body and mind, or as something separate from the body and mind; there is no other possibility. We contemplate this carefully until we become convinced that this is the case and then we proceed to examine each of the four possibilities:

1 If the I is the body, there is no sense in saying 'my body', because the possessor and the possessed are identical.

   If the I is the body, there is no rebirth because the I ceases when the body dies.

   If the I and the body are identical, then since we are capable of developing faith, dreaming, solving mathematical puzzles, and so on, it follows that flesh, blood, and bones can do the same.

   Since none of this is true, it follows that the I is not the body.

2 If the I is the mind, there is no sense in saying 'my mind', because the possessor and the possessed are identical; but usually when we focus on our mind we say 'my mind'. This clearly indicates that the I is not the mind.

   If the I is the mind, then since each person has many types of mind, such as the six consciousnesses, conceptual minds, and non-conceptual minds, it follows that each person has just as many I's. Since this is absurd, it follows that the I is not the mind.

3 Since the body is not the I and the mind is not the I, the collection of the body and mind cannot be the I. The collection of the body and mind is a collection of things that are not the I, so how can the collection itself be the I? For example, in a herd of cows none of the animals is a sheep, therefore the herd itself is not sheep. In the same way, in the collection of the body and mind, neither the body nor the mind is the I, therefore the collection itself is not the I.

You may find this point difficult to understand, but if you think about it for a long time with a calm and positive mind, and discuss it with more experienced practitioners, it will gradually become clear to you. You can also consult authentic books on the subject such as *Heart of Wisdom*.

4 If the I is not the body, not the mind, and not the collection of the body and mind, the only possibility that remains is that it is something separate from the body and mind. If this is the case, we must be able to apprehend the I without either the body or the mind appearing, but if we imagine that our body and our mind were completely to disappear there would be nothing remaining that could be called the I. Therefore it follows that the I is not separate from the body and mind.

We should imagine that our body gradually dissolves into thin air, and then our mind dissolves, our thoughts scatter with the wind, our feelings, wishes, and awareness melt into nothingness. Is there anything left that is the I? There is nothing. Clearly the I is not something separate from the body and mind.

We have now examined all four possibilities and have failed to find the I. Since we have already decided that there is no fifth possibility, we must conclude that the truly existent, or inherently existent I that normally appears so vividly does not exist at all. Where there previously appeared an inherently existent I, there now appears an absence of that I. This absence of an inherently existent I is emptiness, ultimate truth.

FIRST MEDITATION

We contemplate in this way until there appears to our mind a generic image of the absence of an inherently existent I. This image is our object of placement meditation. We try to become completely familiar with it by concentrating on it single-pointedly for as long as possible.

Because we have grasped at an inherently existent I since beginningless time, and have cherished it more dearly than anything else, the experience of failing to find the I in meditation can be quite shocking at first. Some people develop fear, thinking that they have become completely non-existent. Others feel great joy, as if the source of all their problems is vanishing. Both reactions are good signs and indicate correct meditation. After a while, these initial reactions will subside and our mind will settle into a more balanced state. Then we shall be able to meditate on emptiness in a calm, controlled manner.

We should allow our mind to become absorbed in space-like emptiness for as long as possible. It is important to remember that our object is emptiness, the absence of an inherently existent I, not mere nothingness. Occasionally we should check our meditation with alertness. If our mind has wandered to another object, or if we have lost the meaning of emptiness and are focusing on mere nothingness, we should return to the contemplations to bring emptiness clearly to mind once again.

We may wonder 'If there is no truly existent I, then who is meditating? Who will get up from meditation, speak to others, and reply when my name is called?' Though there is nothing within the body and mind, or separate from the body and mind, that is the I, this does not mean that the I does not exist at all. Although the I does not exist in any of the four ways mentioned above, it does exist conventionally. The I is merely a designation imputed by the conceptual mind upon the collection of the body and mind. So long as we are satisfied with the mere designation 'I', there is no problem. We can think 'I exist', 'I am going to town', and so on. The problem arises only when we look for an I other than the mere conceptual imputation, 'I'. The self-grasping mind grasps at an I that ultimately exists, independent of conceptual imputation, as if there were a 'real' I existing behind the label. If such an I existed we would be able to find it, but we have seen that the I cannot be found upon investigation. The conclusion of our search was a definite non-finding of the I. This unfindability of the I is the emptiness of the I, the ultimate nature of the I. The I that exists as mere imputation is the conventional nature of the I.

SECOND CONTEMPLATION

The emptiness of the body

Identifying the object of negation

The way to meditate on the emptiness of the body is similar to the way we meditate on the emptiness of the I. First we must identify the object of negation.

Normally when we think 'my body', a body that exists from its own side and is a single entity not depending upon its parts, appears to our mind. Such a body is the object of negation and is non-existent. 'Truly existent body', 'inherently existent body', and 'body that exists from its own side' all have the same meaning, and all are objects of negation.

Refuting the object of negation

If the body exists as it appears, it must exist in one of two ways: as its parts or separate from its parts; there is no third possibility.

If the body is one with its parts, is it the individual parts or the collection of its parts? If it is the individual parts, then is it the hands, the face, the skin, the bones, the flesh, or the internal organs? By checking carefully 'Is the head the body? Is the flesh the body?' and so on, we shall easily see that none of the individual parts of the body is the body.

If the body is not its individual parts, is it the collection of its parts? The collection of the parts of the body cannot be the body. Why? The parts of the body are all non-bodies, so how can a collection of non-bodies be a body? The hands, feet, and so forth are all parts of the body, but not the body itself. Even though all these parts are assembled together, this collection remains simply parts; it does not magically transform into the part-possessor, the body.

We should recall how our body appears to us when it is praised or insulted. It appears to be, from its own side, a distinct unit. It does not appear as something that is merely designated as a unit but which is in fact made up of many separate parts, like a forest or a herd of cows. Although the body appears as a single entity that exists from its own side without depending upon the limbs, trunk, and head, in reality it is merely designated to the collection of these parts. The collection of the parts of the body is an aggregation of many distinct elements that function together. This aggregation may be thought of as a unit, but that unit has no existence independent of its constituent parts.

If the body is not its parts, the only other possibility is that it is separate from its parts; but if all the parts of the body were to disappear there would be nothing left that could be called the body. We should imagine that all the parts of our body melt into light and disappear. First the skin dissolves, then the flesh, blood, and internal organs, and finally the skeleton melts and vanishes into light. Is there anything left that is our body? There is nothing. There is no body separate from its parts.

We have now exhausted all possibilities. The body is not its parts and it is not separate from its parts. Clearly, the body cannot be found. Where previously there appeared an inherently existent body, there now appears an absence of that body. This absence of an inherently existent body is the emptiness of the body.

SECOND MEDITATION

Recognizing this absence to be the lack of an inherently existent body, we meditate on it single-pointedly. Once again, we should examine our meditation with alertness to make sure that we are meditating on the emptiness of the body and not on nothingness. If we lose the meaning of emptiness, we should return to the contemplations to restore it.

As with the I, the fact that the body cannot be found upon investigation does not imply that the body does not exist at all. The body does exist, but only as a conventional imputation. In accordance with accepted convention, we can impute 'body' to the assembly of limbs, trunk, and head; but if we try to pinpoint the body, hoping to find a substantially existent phenomenon to which the word 'body' refers, we find no body. This unfindability of the body is the emptiness of the body, the ultimate nature of the body. The body that exists as mere imputation is the conventional nature of the body.

Although it is incorrect to assert that the body is identical with the collection of the limbs, trunk, and head, there is no fault in saying that the body is imputed upon this collection. Even though the parts of the body are plural, the body is singular. 'Body' is simply an imputation made by the mind that imputes it. It does not exist from the object's side. There is no fault in imputing a singular phenomenon to a group of many things. For example, we can impute the singular 'forest' to a group of many trees, or 'herd' to a group of many cows.

All phenomena exist by way of convention; nothing is inherently existent. This applies to mind, Buddha, and even to emptiness itself. Everything is merely imputed by mind. All phenomena have parts because physical phenomena have physical parts, and non-physical phenomena have various attributes that can be distinguished by thought. Using the same type of reasoning as above, we can realize that any phenomenon is not one of its parts, not the collection of its parts, and not separate from its parts. In this way we can realize the emptiness of all phenomena.

It is particularly helpful to meditate on the emptiness of objects that arouse in us strong delusions such as attachment or anger. By analyzing correctly we shall realize that the object we desire, or the object we dislike, does not exist from its own side – its beauty or ugliness, and even its very existence, are imputed by mind. By thinking in this way we shall discover that there is no basis for attachment or anger.

DEDICATION

We dedicate all the virtues we have created in this meditation practice to the welfare of all living beings by reciting the dedication prayers.

SUBSEQUENT PRACTICE

During the meditation break we should try to recognize that whatever appears to our mind lacks true existence. In a dream things appear vividly to the dreamer, but when the dreamer wakes he or she immediately realizes that the objects that appeared in the dream were just mental appearances that did not exist from their own side. We should view all phenomena in a similar way. Though they appear vividly to our mind, they lack inherent existence.

Geshe Kelsang Gyatso Rinpoche

Conclusion

Having developed a good heart towards all living beings, we should engage in the Bodhisattva's way of life by keeping the Bodhisattva vows and practising the six perfections. In particular, we should train in the union of tranquil abiding and superior seeing observing emptiness. By practising in this way we shall gradually progress from being an ordinary person to becoming a Bodhisattva. Finally we shall become a fully enlightened being, a Buddha.

Appendix I

A SPECIAL BREATHING MEDITATION

Generally, the purpose of breathing meditation is to calm the mind and reduce distractions before engaging in a practical meditation such as any of the twenty-one meditations described in this book. A simple breathing meditation such as the one explained on page 18 will help us to do this, but the meditation explained here also performs many other functions. It helps us to improve our motivation, to develop a good heart and a controlled mind, and to increase our energy for practising Dharma. It is also a special method for ripening our Buddha seeds, and for preparing us for Highest Yoga Tantra meditation.

In this meditation we combine our breathing with the recitation of the mantra OM AH HUM, which is called the 'mantra of all Buddhas'. There are many different mantras, but they are all contained within these three letters. All Buddhas are contained within three groups: vajra body, vajra speech, and vajra mind. The mantra of vajra body is OM, the mantra of vajra speech is AH, and the mantra of vajra mind is HUM. Therefore if we recite these three letters with faith we shall receive the blessings of the body, speech, and mind of all Buddhas.

A Buddha is someone who is completely free from all faults and limitations, and who has developed all good qualities to perfection. Therefore a Buddha possesses special qualities of body, speech, and mind that are not possessed by ordinary beings. When we recite this mantra we should have deep faith in these qualities, and generate a strong wish to develop them ourself.

Even the most exalted ordinary beings such as kings and queens possess only one body, but a Buddha possesses many bodies. A Buddha's actual body is his omniscient mind. This is called the 'Truth Body'. Because only other enlightened beings can see this body, the Truth Body manifests a subtle Form Body called the 'Enjoyment Body'. This body, however, is very subtle, and can be seen only by Superior Bodhisattvas, those who have a direct realization of emptiness. To be able to communicate directly with ordinary beings, the Enjoyment Body emanates countless gross Form Bodies called 'Emanation Bodies'. There are two types of Emanation Body: Supreme Emanation Bodies and Emanation Bodies appearing as ordinary beings. The former can be seen only by those with pure minds and pure karma, but the latter can be seen by anyone. According to Mahayana Buddhism, Buddha's Emanation Bodies pervade the whole world, although they are not usually recognized by ordinary beings. Ordinary beings have ordinary minds, and so they see everything, even an emanation of Buddha, as ordinary.

A Buddha's speech also possesses many good qualities. Unlike the speech of ordinary beings, which does not have much power, the speech of a Buddha has the power to help all living beings. Everyone wishes to be free from suffering and to experience pure happiness, and Buddha's speech explains how to fulfil this wish. Even though we are constantly seeking happiness, we never find it. Buddha explains that this is because we are trapped in samsara. True happiness can be found only outside samsara. If we want to experience this happiness we must escape from samsara by relying upon the spiritual paths taught by Buddha. Then we shall experience a permanent cessation of suffering, and uninterrupted peace and happiness. Buddha's speech, therefore, is the key that releases us from the prison of samsara and fulfils our wish for happiness.

Buddhas also possess many unique qualities of mind. A Buddha's mind is completely free from ignorance and its imprints, like a sky free from clouds. Because their minds are utterly unobstructed, Buddhas know directly and simultaneously all phenomena of the past, present, and future. The mind of a Buddha is the highest level of mental development.

We all have the seeds of a Buddha's body, speech, and mind; and if we practise pure spiritual paths we can cause these seeds to ripen and accomplish these special qualities. If we continue to improve our present minds of love, compassion, and bodhichitta, we shall become a Bodhisattva. If we then continue to train in pure spiritual paths, eventually we shall become a Buddha. In Mahayana Buddhism our way of relying upon Buddha is not simply asking Buddha to help us, but striving ourself to become a Buddha to be able to help others. Therefore we should try gradually to reduce our faults of body, speech, and mind, and to develop all good qualities instead. As our faults diminish and our good qualities increase we shall come closer and closer to Buddhahood. Eventually we shall become a fully enlightened being. Many thousands of Mahayana practitioners in the past have attained enlightenment in this way.

Contemplating these points we should think:

How wonderful it would be if I became a Buddha and attained the good qualities of a Buddha's body, speech, and mind! At the moment I have no power to help others, but if I become a Buddha I shall be able to help all living beings without exception. Therefore I must become a Buddha.

This motivation is bodhichitta. With this motivation we should engage in the recitation of the mantra OM AH HUM, while remembering its meaning. Until we become used to the mantra we should recite it verbally; then we can combine it with breathing meditation.

To do this we breathe gently and naturally through both nostrils. As we inhale we mentally recite OM. We then hold the breath briefly at our heart and mentally recite AH. Then, as we gently exhale, we mentally recite HUM. We repeat this cycle as many times as we wish, all the time remembering the meaning of the mantra with a mind of faith. The 'heart' that is referred to here is the spiritual heart, not the physical heart. It is located in the centre of the chest. To begin with we shall be able to hold our breath only for a short time, but with familiarity we shall be able to hold it for longer and longer without discomfort.

This meditation produces many good results. It calms our mind and causes our distracting conceptions to sub-side. It strengthens the life-supporting wind at our heart, thereby increasing our lifespan and protecting us from premature death. Because we do this meditation with the motivation to attain the good qualities of a Buddha's body, speech, and mind, we are also training in bodhi-chitta, accumulating merit, and receiving Buddha's bless-ings. It causes our Buddha seeds to ripen, and it prepares us for Highest Yoga Tantra meditation, making it easy to attain completion stage realizations in the future. There-fore, it is far more powerful than ordinary breathing meditation.

The effects of this practice remain even when we rise from meditation. If we do this meditation regularly we shall find that our mind gradually becomes more positive and more controlled. It will become like a well-trained horse that does whatever the rider wishes. If we wish to meditate, our mind will remain on the object without distraction. If we wish to do prostrations, it will engage happily, without procrastination or laziness. As our mind becomes more controlled we shall find it easier to refrain from negative actions of body, speech, and mind, and to practise virtue. We shall experience peace and happiness day and night, in life after life; and be able to share the benefits of this experience with others. This is the real meaning of the Buddhist way of life.

Understanding the many benefits of this special breathing meditation, we should try to do it whenever we can.

Appendix II

When we go for refuge we undertake to observe twelve special commitments. By observing these sincerely we protect our mind of refuge, and it gradually becomes more powerful. These commitments lay the foundation for all the realizations of the stages of the path. Realizing this, we should not regard them as a burden, but practise them joyfully and sincerely.

Within the twelve commitments there are six specific commitments and six general commitments. The six specific commitments are so called because they are related specifically to each of the Three Jewels. There are two commitments related to Buddha, two related to Dharma, and two related to Sangha. In each case there is one thing to abandon and one thing to practise. The remaining six commitments apply equally to Buddha, Dharma, and Sangha. These twelve commitments will now be briefly explained.

THE TWO COMMITMENTS SPECIFICALLY
RELATED TO BUDDHA

1 Not to go for refuge to teachers who contradict Buddha's view, or to samsaric gods. By going for refuge to Buddha we have a commitment to abandon going for ultimate refuge to teachers who contradict Buddha's view, or to worldly gods. This does not mean that we cannot receive help from others; it means that we do not rely upon others to provide ultimate protection from suffering.

2 To regard any image of Buddha as an actual Buddha. By going for refuge to Buddha we also have a commitment to regard any image of Buddha as an actual Buddha. Whenever we see a statue of Buddha, whether it is made of gold or anything else, we should see it as an actual Buddha. We should disregard the material or the quality of the craftsmanship, and pay homage by making offerings and prostrations, and by going for refuge. If we practise like this our merit will increase abundantly.

THE TWO COMMITMENTS SPECIFICALLY
RELATED TO DHARMA

3 Not to harm others. By going for refuge to Dharma we have a commitment to abandon harming others. Instead of treating others badly we should try, with the best motivation, to benefit them whenever we can. We first need to concentrate on reducing harmful thoughts and generating a beneficial intention towards those who are close to us, such as our friends and family. When we have developed a good heart towards these people we can gradually extend our practice to include more and more people, until finally we have a good heart towards all living beings. If we can abandon harmful thoughts and always have a beneficial intention, we shall easily attain the realizations of great love and great compassion. In this way we begin to increase our compassion, which is the very essence of Buddhadharma, from the very beginning of our practice of going for refuge.

4 To regard all Dharma scriptures as the actual Dharma Jewel. By going for refuge to Dharma we also have a commitment to regard all Dharma scriptures as the actual Dharma Jewel. Dharma is the source of all health and happiness. Since we cannot see actual Dharma Jewels with our eyes, we need to regard Dharma texts as actual Dharma Jewels. Actual Dharma Jewels arise only as a result of learning, contemplating, and meditating on the meaning of the scriptures. We need to respect every letter of the scriptures, and every letter of explanation of Buddha's teaching. Therefore, we must treat Dharma books with great care and avoid walking over them or putting them in inappropriate places where they might be damaged or misused. Each time we neglect or spoil our Dharma books we create the cause to become more ignorant because these actions are similar to the action of abandoning Dharma. Once the great Tibetan Teacher Geshe Sharawa saw some people playing carelessly with their Dharma books and he said to them 'You should not do that. You already have enough ignorance. Why do you want to make yourselves even more ignorant?'

THE TWO COMMITMENTS SPECIFICALLY
RELATED TO SANGHA

5 Not to allow ourself to be influenced by people who reject Buddha's teaching. By going for refuge to Sangha we have a commitment to stop being influenced by people who reject Buddha's teaching. This does not mean that we should abandon these people, merely that we should not let their views influence our mind. Without abandoning love and consideration for others, we need to be vigilant and make sure that we are not being led astray by their bad habits and unsound advice.

6 To regard anyone who wears the robes of an ordained person as an actual Sangha Jewel. By going for refuge to Sangha we also have a commitment to acknowledge anyone who wears the robes of an ordained person as an actual Sangha Jewel. Even if ordained Sangha are poor, we still need to pay respect to them because they are keeping moral discipline, and this is something very rare and precious.

7 To go for refuge to the Three Jewels again and again, remembering their good qualities and the differences between them. Dharma is like a boat that can carry us across the ocean of samsara, Buddha is like the skilful navigator of the boat, and the Sangha are like the crew. Remembering this, we should go for refuge again and again to the Three Jewels.

8 To offer the first portion of whatever we eat and drink to the Three Jewels, while remembering their kindness. Since we need to eat and drink several times each day, if we always offer the first portion of our food or drink to the Three Jewels remembering their kindness, we shall greatly increase our merit. We can do this with the following prayer:

I make this offering to you, Buddha Shakyamuni,
Whose mind is the synthesis of all Buddha Jewels,
Whose speech is the synthesis of all Dharma Jewels,
Whose body is the synthesis of all Sangha Jewels.
O Blessed One, please accept this and bless my
   mind.

OM AH HUM   (3x)

It is important always to remember Buddha's kindness. All our happiness is a result of Buddha's kindness because all Buddha's actions are pervaded by compassion and concern for others, and it is these actions that enable us to perform virtuous actions that are the cause of our happiness.

Without Buddha's kindness we would not know the real causes of happiness, or the real causes of suffering. Buddha taught us how all happiness and suffering depend upon the mind. He showed us how to abandon those states of mind that cause suffering and cultivate those states of mind that cause happiness. In other words, he taught us perfect methods for overcoming suffering and attaining happiness. No one else taught us these methods. How kind Buddha is!

Our own human body is proof of Buddha's kindness. It is by virtue of Buddha's blessings and instructions that we were able to create the cause to take rebirth in a human form, with all the freedoms and endowments necessary for spiritual practice. If we are now able to learn Dharma and meet Spiritual Guides, it is only through Buddha's kindness. We can now practise the methods that lead to full enlightenment and gain spiritual realizations only because Buddha was kind enough to turn the Wheel of Dharma and show his example in this world. Even the small wisdom we possess to discriminate between what is beneficial and what is harmful, and to identify Buddha's teaching as worthwhile, is a result of Buddha's kindness.

We should not think that Buddha helps only those who follow him. Buddha attained enlightenment to benefit all living beings. He manifests in many different forms, sometimes even as non-Buddhist teachers, to help others. There is no living being who has not benefited from the kindness of Buddha.

9 With compassion, always to encourage others to go for refuge. We should always try to help others to go for refuge, but we should do so skilfully. If we know someone who is interested in Dharma we should help them to develop the causes of going for refuge: fear of suffering and faith in the Three Jewels. We can talk to them about impermanence – how the conditions of this life change and how our body will grow old and decay – and we can talk about the sufferings of ageing, sickness, and death. We can talk about what will happen after death, about the different types of rebirth, and about how all types of rebirth are in the nature of suffering. If we skilfully introduce these things into our conversations, the other person will begin to lose his complacency and, when he starts to feel uneasy, he will naturally want to find out what can be done. At this point we can explain about Buddha, Dharma, and Sangha, and how they can help us. Then we can explain how to go for refuge.

If we help someone else tactfully in this way, without being arrogant or impatient, we shall bring them real benefit. It is never certain that the material gifts we give to others will actually help them; sometimes they even cause more problems. The best way to help others is to lead them into Dharma. If we cannot give elaborate explanations, we can at least give proper advice to those who are unhappy, and help them to solve their problems by means of Dharma.

10 To go for refuge at least three times during the day and three times during the night, remembering the benefits of going for refuge. So that we never forget the Three Jewels we should go for refuge once every four hours, or at least three times during the day and three times during the night. If we never forget the Three Jewels and regularly contemplate the benefits of going for refuge, we shall gain realizations very quickly. We should be like a businessman who never forgets his projects even while he is relaxing.

11 To perform every action with complete trust in the Three Jewels. We should rely upon the Three Jewels in everything that we do. In this way all our actions will be successful. There is no need to seek the inspiration and blessings of worldly gods, but we should always try to receive the blessings of Buddha, Dharma, and Sangha by making offerings and requests.

12 Never to forsake the Three Jewels, even at the cost of our life, or as a joke. We should never abandon the Three Jewels because going for refuge is the foundation of all Dharma realizations. Once a Buddhist was taken captive and his enemy said to him 'Give up your refuge in Buddha or I will kill you.' He refused to forsake his refuge and was killed, but when clairvoyants looked they saw that he had immediately been reborn as a god.

Appendix III

A SUGGESTED RETREAT SCHEDULE

When we do retreat on the twenty-one meditations it is best if our retreat is at least one week long. If possible we should do four sessions each day. The first session should be early in the morning, the second before lunch, the third in the late afternoon, and the fourth in the evening. We can make the sessions as long as we wish, from half an hour up to two hours each. We should begin each session with the preparatory practices and then engage in the contemplations and meditations according to the sequence suggested below. At the end of each session we should dedicate our merit for the welfare of all living beings, and in between sessions we should try to engage in the subsequent practices with strong mindfulness. If the retreat is longer than one week we can repeat the cycle each week. In this way, each week we shall cover all twenty-one meditations, from relying upon a Spiritual Guide to superior seeing.

DAY ONE

Session 1   Meditation 1 – Relying upon a Spiritual Guide
Session 2   Meditation 2 – Our precious human life
Session 3   Meditation 3 – Death and impermanence
Session 4   Meditations 4, 5, & 6 – The danger of lower rebirth, refuge practice, and actions and their effects

DAY TWO

Session 1	Meditation 7 – Developing renunciation, using the first four contemplations: birth, ageing, sickness, and death
Session 2	Meditation 7 – Developing renunciation, using the remaining three contemplations
Session 3	Meditation 7 – Developing renunciation, using all seven contemplations
Session 4	Meditation 7 – Developing renunciation, using all seven contemplations

DAY THREE

Session 1	Meditation 8 – Developing equanimity
Session 2	Meditation 9 – Recognizing that all living beings are our mothers
Session 3	Meditation 10 – Remembering the kindness of living beings
Session 4	Meditation 11 – Equalizing self and others

DAY FOUR

Session 1	Meditation 12 – The disadvantages of self-cherishing
Session 2	Meditation 13 – The advantages of cherishing others
Session 3	Meditation 14 – Exchanging self with others
Session 4	Meditation 15 – Great compassion

DAY FIVE

Session 1	Meditation 16 – Taking
Session 2	Meditation 17 – Wishing love
Session 3	Meditation 18 – Giving
Session 4	Meditation 19 – Bodhichitta

DAY SIX

All four sessions Meditation 20 – Tranquil abiding, using either our chosen object or bodhichitta as our meditation object

DAY SEVEN

All four sessions Meditation 21 – Superior seeing, meditation on emptiness

Glossary

Alertness A mental factor that is a type of wisdom that examines our activity of body, speech, and mind and knows whether or not faults are developing.

Aspiring bodhichitta A bodhichitta that is a mere wish to attain enlightenment for the benefit of all living beings. See also *Bodhichitta*.

Blessing The transformation of our mind from a negative state to a positive state, from an unhappy state to a happy state, or from a state of weakness to a state of strength, through the inspiration of holy beings such as our Spiritual Guide, Buddhas, and Bodhisattvas.

Bodhichitta Sanskrit word for 'mind of enlightenment'. 'Bodhi' means enlightenment, and 'chitta' means mind. There are two types of bodhichitta: conventional bodhichitta and ultimate bodhichitta. Generally speaking, the term 'bodhichitta' refers to conventional bodhichitta, which is a primary mind motivated by great compassion that spontaneously seeks enlightenment to benefit all living beings. Conventional bodhichitta is of two types: aspiring bodhichitta and engaging bodhichitta. Ultimate bodhichitta is a wisdom motivated by conventional bodhichitta that directly realizes emptiness, the ultimate nature of phenomena. See also *Aspiring bodhichitta* and *Engaging bodhichitta*. See *Joyful Path, Meaningful to Behold*, and *Universal Compassion*.

Bodhisattva A person who has generated spontaneous bodhichitta but who has not yet become a Buddha. From the moment a practitioner generates a non-artificial, or spontaneous, bodhichitta he or she becomes a Bodhisattva and enters the first Mahayana path, the path of accumulation.

An ordinary Bodhisattva is one who has not realized emptiness directly, and a Superior Bodhisattva is one who has attained a direct realization of emptiness. See *Joyful Path* and *Meaningful to Behold*.

Buddha A being who has completely abandoned all delusions and their imprints. There are many beings who have become Buddhas in the past, and there are many who will become Buddhas in the future. See *Joyful Path*.

Buddha seed The root mind of a sentient being, and its ultimate nature. Buddha seed, Buddha lineage, and Buddha nature are synonyms. All sentient beings have Buddha seed and therefore have the potential to attain Buddhahood.

Buddha Shakyamuni The fourth of one thousand Buddhas who are to appear in this world during this Fortunate Aeon. The first three were Krakuchchanda, Kanakamuni, and Kashyapa. The fifth Buddha will be Maitreya.

Buddhadharma See *Dharma*.

Changing suffering For samsaric beings, every experience of happiness or pleasure that arises from samsara's enjoyments is changing suffering, because these experiences are contaminated and have the nature of suffering. See *Joyful Path*.

Clairvoyance Abilities that arise from special concentration. There are five principal types of clairvoyance: eye clairvoyance (the ability to see subtle and distant forms), ear clairvoyance (the ability to hear subtle and distant sounds), remembering former lives, knowing others' minds, and the clairvoyance of miracle powers (the ability to emanate various forms by mind). Some beings, such as bardo beings and some humans and spirits, have contaminated clairvoyance that is developed due to karma, but these are not actual clairvoyance.

Completion stage Highest Yoga Tantra realizations that are attained through completing a special method that causes the winds to enter, abide, and dissolve within the central channel. See *Clear Light of Bliss*, *Tantric Grounds and Paths*, *Great Treasury of Merit*, and *Guide to Dakini Land*.

Conscientiousness A mental factor that, in dependence upon effort, cherishes what is virtuous and guards the mind from delusion and non-virtue. See *Joyful Path*, *Meaningful to Behold*, and *Understanding the Mind*.

Delusion A mental factor that arises from inappropriate attention and functions to make the mind unpeaceful and uncontrolled. There are three main delusions: ignorance, attachment, and hatred. From these, all other delusions such as jealousy, pride, and deluded doubt arise. See *Joyful Path* and *Understanding the Mind*.

Dharma Buddha's teachings and the inner realizations attained by practising them.

Emptiness Lack of inherent existence, the ultimate nature of all phenomena. See *Heart of Wisdom*, *Joyful Path*, and *Ocean of Nectar*.

Energy winds See *Inner winds*.

Engaging bodhichitta A bodhichitta held by the Bodhisattva vows. See also *Bodhichitta*.

Enlightenment Usually the full enlightenment of Buddhahood. There are three levels of enlightenment: small enlightenment, or the enlightenment of a Hearer; middling enlightenment, or the enlightenment of a Solitary Conqueror; and great enlightenment, or the enlightenment of a Buddha. An enlightenment is a liberation and a true cessation. See *Clear Light of Bliss*, *Joyful Path*, *Ocean of Nectar*, and *Tantric Grounds and Paths*.

Generic image The appearing object of a conceptual mind. See *Heart of Wisdom* and *Understanding the Mind*.

Geshe Langri Tangpa (AD 1054–1123) A great Kadampa Geshe who was famous for his realization of exchanging self with others. He composed *Eight Verses of Training the Mind*.

Giving A virtuous mental decision to give, or a bodily or verbal action of giving that is motivated by a virtuous state of mind. There are three types of giving: giving material things, giving Dharma, and giving fearlessness. See *Joyful Path* and *Introduction to Buddhism*.

Guru Sanskrit word for Spiritual Guide. See also *Spiritual Guide*.

Highest Yoga Tantra A Tantric instruction that includes the method for transforming sexual experience into the spiritual path. See *Great Treasury of Merit*, *Guide to Dakini Land*, *Clear Light of Bliss*, and *Tantric Grounds and Paths*.

Hinayana Sanskrit word for 'Lesser Vehicle'. The Hinayana goal is to attain merely one's own liberation from suffering by completely abandoning delusions. See *Joyful Path*.

Inner winds Special winds related to the mind that flow through the channels of our body. Our mind cannot function without these winds. See *Clear Light of Bliss*, *Tantric Grounds and Paths*, and *Great Treasury of Merit*.

Intermediate state 'Bardo' in Tibetan. The state between death and rebirth. It begins the moment the consciousness leaves the body and ceases the moment the consciousness enters the body of the next life. See *Joyful Path* and *Clear Light of Bliss*.

Kadampa A person who sincerely practises Lamrim, and who integrates all the teachings of Buddha that he or she knows into their Lamrim practice.

Karma Sanskrit term referring to actions and their effects. Through the force of intention we perform actions with our body, speech, and mind, and all of these actions produce effects. The effect of virtuous actions is happiness and the effect of negative actions is suffering. See *Joyful Path*.

Lamrim Literally, 'the stages of the path'. A special arrangement of all Buddha's teachings that is easy to understand and put into practice. It reveals all the stages of the path to enlightenment.

Liberation Complete freedom from samsara and its cause, the delusions. See *Joyful Path*.

Lineage A line of instruction that has been handed down from Teacher to disciple, with each Guru in the line having gained personal experience of the instructions before passing them on to others.

Living being See *Sentient being*.

Lojong See *Training the mind*.

Mahayana Sanskrit word for 'Great Vehicle', the spiritual path to great enlightenment. See *Joyful Path* and *Meaningful to Behold*.

Mantra Literally, 'mind protection'. Mantra protects the mind from ordinary appearances and conceptions. See *Heart of Wisdom*, *Guide to Dakini Land*, and *Tantric Grounds and Paths*.

Mental image See *Generic image*.

Mental suppleness A flexibility of mind induced by virtuous concentration. See *Clear Light of Bliss*, *Joyful Path*, and *Understanding the Mind*.

Merit The good fortune created by virtuous actions. It is the potential power to increase our good qualities and produce happiness.

Mindfulness A mental factor that functions not to forget the object realized by the primary mind. See *Clear Light of Bliss*, *Joyful Path*, *Meaningful to Behold*, and *Understanding the Mind*.

Miracle powers See *Clairvoyance*.

Nine mental abidings Nine levels of concentration leading to tranquil abiding. They are: placing the mind, continual placement, replacement, close placement, controlling, pacifying, completely pacifying, single-pointedness, and placement in equipoise. See *Meaningful to Behold*, *Joyful Path*, and *Clear Light of Bliss*.

Non-virtuous actions The ten non-virtuous actions are: killing, stealing, sexual misconduct, lying, divisive speech, hurtful speech, idle gossip, covetousness, malice, and holding wrong view. See *Joyful Path* and *Meaningful to Behold*.

Pure Land A pure environment in which there are no true sufferings. There are many Pure Lands. For example, Tushita is the Pure Land of Buddha Maitreya; Sukhavati is the Pure Land of Buddha Amitabha; and Dakini Land, or Keajra, is the Pure Land of Buddha Vajrayogini. See *Guide to Dakini Land* and *Heart Jewel*.

Purification Generally, any practice that leads to the attainment of a pure body, speech, or mind. More specifically, a practice for purifying negative karma. See *Joyful Path*, *The Bodhisattva Vow*, *Universal Compassion*, and *Guide to Dakini Land*.

Realization A stable and non-mistaken experience of a virtuous object that directly protects us from suffering.

Sangha According to the Vinaya tradition, any community of four or more fully-ordained monks or nuns. In general, ordained or lay people who take Bodhisattva vows or Tantric vows can also be said to be Sangha.

Self-cherishing A mental attitude that considers oneself to be precious or important. It is regarded as a principal object to be abandoned by Bodhisattvas. See *Universal Compassion*, *Joyful Path*, and *Meaningful to Behold*.

Self-grasping A conceptual mind that holds any phenomenon to be inherently existent. The mind of self-grasping gives rise to all other delusions such as anger and attachment. It is the root cause of all suffering and dissatisfaction. See *Joyful Path*, *Heart of Wisdom*, and *Ocean of Nectar*.

Sentient being Any being who possesses a mind that is contaminated by delusions or their imprints. Both 'sentient being' and 'living being' are terms used to distinguish beings whose minds are contaminated by either of the two obstructions from Buddhas, whose minds are completely free from these obstructions.

Sevenfold cause and effect A method for generating bodhichitta in which affectionate love is developed primarily by recognizing all sentient beings as our mothers and remembering their kindness. See *Joyful Path* and *Meaningful to Behold*.

Six perfections The perfections of giving, moral discipline, patience, effort, mental stabilization, and wisdom. They are called perfections because they are motivated by bodhichitta. See *Joyful Path*, *Meaningful to Behold*, *The Bodhisattva Vow*, and *Ocean of Nectar*.

Spiritual Guide Any Teacher who guides us along the spiritual path. See *Joyful Path*, *Great Treasury of Merit*, and *Heart Jewel*.

Stages of the path See *Lamrim*.

Superior seeing A special wisdom that sees its object clearly, and that is maintained by tranquil abiding and the special suppleness that is induced by investigation. See *Joyful Path*.

Suppleness See *Mental suppleness*.

Three Jewels The three objects of refuge: Buddha Jewel, Dharma Jewel, and Sangha Jewel. They are called 'Jewels' because they are both rare and precious. See *Joyful Path*.

Training the mind 'Lojong' in Tibetan. A special lineage of instructions deriving from Manjushri and passed down through Shantideva, Atisha, and the Kadampa Geshes, that emphasizes the generation of bodhichitta through the practices of equalizing and exchanging self with others combined with taking and giving. See *Universal Compassion*, *Joyful Path*, and *Meaningful to Behold*.

Tranquil abiding A concentration that possesses the special bliss of suppleness of body and mind that is attained in dependence upon completing the nine mental abidings. See *Clear Light of Bliss*, *Joyful Path*, and *Meaningful to Behold*.

Vajra Generally the Sanskrit word 'vajra' means indestructible like a diamond and powerful like a thunderbolt. In the context of Secret Mantra it means the indivisibility of method and wisdom. See *Tantric Grounds and Paths.*

Vajra posture The perfect cross-legged posture. Buddha Shakyamuni is depicted in this posture on the cover of this book.

Valid cognizer A cognizer that is non-deceptive with respect to its engaged object. There are two types: inferential valid cognizers and direct valid cognizers. See *Heart of Wisdom* and *Understanding the Mind.*

Vows Promises to refrain from certain actions. The three sets of vows are the Pratimoksha vows of individual liberation, the Bodhisattva vows, and the Secret Mantra vows. See *The Bodhisattva Vow* and *Guide to Dakini Land.*

Wishfulfilling jewel A legendary jewel that grants whatever is wished for.

Bibliography

Geshe Kelsang Gyatso is a highly respected meditation master and scholar of the Mahayana Buddhist tradition founded by Je Tsong-khapa. Since arriving in the UK in 1977, Geshe Kelsang has worked tirelessly to establish pure Kadampa Buddhism throughout the world. Over this period he has given extensive teachings on the major scriptures of the Mahayana. These teachings are currently being published and provide a comprehensive presentation of the essential Sutra and Tantra practices of Mahayana Buddhism.

Books in print

The Bodhisattva Vow. The essential practices of Mahayana Buddhism. (Tharpa, 1991.)

Buddhism in the Tibetan Tradition. A guide to Tibetan Buddhism. (2nd. edn. Penguin, 1990.)

Clear Light of Bliss. A commentary to the practice of Mahamudra in Vajrayana Buddhism. (2nd. edn. Tharpa, 1992.)

Great Treasury of Merit. A commentary to the practice of *Offering to the Spiritual Guide* (*Lama Chöpa*). (Tharpa, 1992.)

Guide to Dakini Land. A commentary to the Highest Yoga Tantra practice of Venerable Vajrayogini. (Tharpa, 1991.)

Heart Jewel. A commentary to the essential practice of the New Kadampa Tradition of Mahayana Buddhism. (Tharpa, 1991.)

Heart of Wisdom. A commentary to the *Heart Sutra.* (2nd. edn. Tharpa, 1989.)

Introduction to Buddhism. An explanation of the Buddhist way of life. (Tharpa, 1992.)

Joyful Path of Good Fortune. The stages of the path to enlightenment. (Tharpa, 1990.)

Meaningful to Behold. The Bodhisattva's way of life. (4th. edn. Tharpa, 1994.)

Tantric Grounds and Paths. How to enter, progress on, and complete the Vajrayana path. (Tharpa, 1994.)

Understanding the Mind. Lorig – An explanation of the nature and functions of the mind. (Tharpa, 1993.)

Universal Compassion. A commentary to Bodhisattva Chekhawa's *Training the Mind in Seven Points.* (2nd. edn. Tharpa, 1993.)

Sadhanas

Geshe Kelsang is also supervising the translation of a collection of essential sadhanas and practical booklets. Those already in print include:

The Bodhisattva's Confession of Moral Downfalls. The purification practice of the *Mahayana Sutra of the Three Superior Heaps.*

Chenrezig Sadhana. Prayers and requests to the Buddha of compassion.

Dakini Yoga: Vajrayogini Six-Session Sadhana. Six-session Guru yoga combined with self-generation as Vajrayogini.

Drop of Essential Nectar. A special fasting and purification practice in conjunction with Eleven-faced Avalokiteshvara.

Essence of Good Fortune. Prayers for the six preparatory practices for meditation on the stages of the path to enlightenment.

Essence of Vajrayana. The condensed meaning of Vajrayana Mahamudra and prayers of request to the lineage Gurus.

Feast of Great Bliss. Vajrayogini self-initiation sadhana.

Great Compassionate Mother. The sadhana of Arya Tara.

Great Liberation of the Mother. Preliminary prayers for Mahamudra meditation in conjunction with Vajrayogini practice.

The Great Mother. A method to overcome hindrances and obstacles by reciting the *Essence of Wisdom Sutra* (the *Heart Sutra*).

Heart Jewel. The Guru yoga of Je Tsongkhapa combined with the condensed sadhana of his Dharma Protector.

The Hundreds of Deities of the Joyful Land. The Guru yoga of Je Tsongkhapa.

The Kadampa Way of Life. Essential practices of the New Kadampa Tradition.

Liberation from Sorrow. Praises and requests to the Twenty-one Taras.

Medicine Guru Sadhana. The method for making requests to the Assembly of Seven Medicine Buddhas.

Meditation and Recitation of Solitary Vajrasattva.

Melodious Drum Victorious in all Directions. The extensive fulfilling and restoring ritual of the Dharma Protector, the great king Dorje Shugdän, in conjunction with Mahakala, Kalarupa, Kalindewi, and other Dharma Protectors.

Offering to the Spiritual Guide. (*Lama Chöpa*). A special Guru yoga practice of Je Tsongkhapa's tradition.

Prayers for Meditation. Brief preparatory prayers for meditation.

A Pure Life. The practice of taking and keeping the eight Mahayana precepts.

The Quick Path. A condensed practice of Heruka Five Deities according to Master Ghantapa's tradition.

Quick Path to Great Bliss. Vajrayogini self-generation sadhana.

Treasury of Wisdom. The sadhana of Venerable Manjushri.

Wishfulfilling Jewel. The Guru yoga of Je Tsongkhapa combined with the sadhana of his Dharma Protector.

The Yoga of Buddha Amitayus. A special method for increasing lifespan, wisdom, and merit.

For a catalogue of books and sadhanas by Geshe Kelsang Gyatso please contact:

Tharpa Publications
Kilnwick Percy Hall
Pocklington
York YO4 2UF
England
Tel: 01759–306446
Fax: 01759–306397

Study Programmes

Geshe Kelsang has prepared three study programmes based on his books, which are designed to fulfil the wishes of those who would like to study Buddhism systematically and thereby deepen their experience of the essential practices.

The **General Programme** provides a basic introduction to Buddhist view, meditation, and action, and various kinds of teaching and practice from both Sutra and Tantra.

The **Foundation Programme** is designed for those who prefer a more structured approach to their spiritual training. Based on five of Geshe Kelsang's books, this programme lasts for approximately four years. The classes consist of readings, teachings, discussions, pujas, and meditations. It is possible to enrol for one subject at a time. Each subject concludes with an examination.

The **Teacher Training Programme** is designed for those who wish to train as authentic Dharma Teachers. This programme, which takes approximately seven years to complete, is based on twelve of Geshe Kelsang's books. To qualify as Dharma Teachers, participants must complete the study of all eleven texts, pass an examination in each subject, satisfy certain criteria with regard to behaviour and lifestyle, and complete various meditation retreats.

These three programmes are taught worldwide at Centres of the New Kadampa Tradition. All these Centres are under the spiritual direction of Geshe Kelsang. The two main Centres are:

Manjushri Centre	**Madhyamaka Centre**
Conishead Priory	Kilnwick Percy Hall
Ulverston	Pocklington
Cumbria, LA12 9QQ	York, YO4 2UF
England	England
Tel: 01229–584029	Tel: 01759–304832
Founded 1975	Founded 1979

Addresses of all the other Centres are available from: James Belither, Secretary, the New Kadampa Tradition (NKT), Conishead Priory, Ulverston, Cumbria, LA12 9QQ, UK. Tel 01229–584029.